Intellectual Development

Also by the Authors

Social and Emotional Development:
Connecting Science and Practice in Early Childhood Settings

Intellectual development

Connecting Science and Practice in Early Childhood Settings

Dave Riley

Mary Carns

Ann Ramminger

Joan Klinkner

Colette Sisco

with

Kathleen Burns

Cindy Clark-Ericksen

Mary A. Roach

Robert R. San Juan

Redleaf Press
www.redleafpress.org
800-423-8309

Published by Redleaf Press
10 Yorkton Court
St. Paul, MN 55117
www.redleafpress.org

First edition 2009
Cover design by Fiona Raven
Cover photographs by Steve Wewerka
Interior typeset in Sabon and composition by Navta Associates Inc.
Printed in the United States of America
15 14 13 12 11 10 09 08   1 2 3 4 5 6 7 8

Library of Congress Cataloging-in-Publication Data
Intellectual development : connecting science and practice in early childhood settings / Dave Riley ... [et al.].
    p. cm.
 Includes bibliographical references and index.
 ISBN 978-1-933653-63-1 (alk. paper)
 1. Early Child education—Activity programs. 2. Cognition in children.
3. Child development. I. Riley, Dave.
 LB1139.35.A37I58 2009
 372.21—dc22

                                                                2008006817

Printed on acid-free paper

This book could not have been written without the support of our families, the wisdom of our teachers, and the many children who have taught us . . . to look, to see, to understand, to appreciate, to love, and most of all, to play. We dedicate this book to all of you, and in particular:

To my ECE teachers, Emily Diaz, Mary Montalvan, Georgie Feeney, and Betty Jones. (DR)

To my first playmate, my sister Becky, and to Ben, Amy, and Noah, who make life fun. (MC)

To Bob, Kyle, Aaron, Nathan, and Beema for support and inspiration. (AR)

To my husband, Mike, and our daughters Lisa and Valerie, for their love and support. (JK)

To my sons Matthew, Ben, and Michael who are my consummate teachers about life. (CS)

To my husband, Jerry, and our daughters Sadie, Sara, Liz, and Erin. (KB)

To my children Emma, Ansel, and Charlotte, who continue to help me grow and learn. (CCE)

To my husband, Jim, and my amazing children, Elizabeth and Thomas. (MR)

To my siblings Maribel, Maricel, and Ron, and also the Harman family: Emma, Chris, and Vanessa. (RSJ)

There is a little piece of each of you within these pages.

Intellectual Development

Introduction

A parent had heard this was a good early childhood center, but she was not impressed when she came to observe and saw the morning activity: the children clapped their hands while singing a silly song, "I like to eat, eat, eat, eeples and beneenies, I like to oat, oat, oat, oples and bononos . . ." The parent asked the teacher, "Don't you do anything educational?"

The teacher didn't know how to respond. She had been taught to do this kind of activity by a highly respected Master Teacher, who had explained that it was important to child development. But the teacher didn't know exactly what part of child development it addressed. She was doing "early childhood education" as she had been taught, and as the children loved it, but she had no understanding of the reasons for "developmentally appropriate practice."

Because this teacher didn't understand the *reasons* for good practice in early education, she was unable to explain the benefits of different classroom activities to either the parent or to her new teacher's assistant. Because she could not interpret her classroom to the parent, the parent was then unlikely to view this classroom as an educational setting (which is a key reason why many parents see no justification for higher fees to pay higher staff wages). If this teacher understood the "why's" behind her practices, she would feel more like a professional teacher, and she would be able to "sell" her program in a way that could lead to more professional wages.

This book was written, in part, to help this teacher answer the parent's question, and the thousand other similar questions we get about our classroom practices. This book explains *why* we do *what* we do in early care and education. The book you are currently reading covers intellectual development. We have also written a companion volume: *Social and Emotional Development: Connecting Science and Practice in Early Childhood Settings.*

In fact, knowing the "why's" underlying our practices also can improve those practices. Many of our most skilled early childhood teachers have honed their skills into an automatic, unconscious pattern of wonderful classroom practices. These teachers are so skilled that they don't have to think about what they are doing. However, if this book makes them more conscious of their skills and how these skills influence child development, then they can exercise those skills more consistently and mentor them to new teachers more easily. Maria Montessori was the first (and Jean Piaget the best) to point this out, that we often learn things unconsciously through our everyday actions. However, if we raise an unconscious skill to the conscious, conceptual level, then we have a new kind of control over the skill and can wield it in a more powerful way.

Knowing the "why's" underlying good practices can be very rewarding to any teacher, and particularly the best teachers. Many of the everyday practices of early care and education can seem hum-drum and unimportant (for example, singing with children, doing art projects, or talking with them about what they are doing). However, the best scientific research of the last two decades has shown conclusively that some of these everyday activities make a huge difference in children's development. These early differences can lead to differences in outcomes across the whole lifespan. Reading this book should give most early childhood teachers a dramatically raised appreciation of the significance of their work. Very few occupations make as large a difference in so many lives.

The ability to explain the "why's" of good practice is also important for another reason. Policy makers are increasingly interested in extending public education into lower ages, beginning with a movement toward publicly funded prekindergarten in many U.S. states. This trend could be very good not only for children, but also for elementary education, because a linkage and partnership could form between early childhood and elementary education programs. Although most of us see the potential benefit of this relationship, we also fear the possibility that the methods of most elementary education programs may simply be extended downward into classrooms for four-year-olds and three-year-olds. Based on what we know of child development, this would benefit neither the children nor society. In our view, elementary education may have more to learn from early care and education programs, about working with young children, than the other way around.

Elementary teachers are often trained in schools of education, which focus more on the curriculum and practice of teaching than on how children learn. If the teacher has a focus on curriculum (the subject matter to be mastered), then providing the same experiences and instruction to the whole class at once seems natural and indeed efficient. If the focus is on curriculum, an individual child's emotions become a distraction from learning, rather than the key to active and motivated learning.

In contrast, the roots of early childhood education lie in a different field of study: not education, but child development. This field begins by asking how children grow and learn. When you are part of this tradition, as most early childhood teachers are, then teaching doesn't start with the curriculum to be mastered, noticing children's deficiencies. Instead, you begin with what the child currently understands, and you build from there. With this perspective, treating every child differently seems natural, as each child approaches the topic with different understandings, learning through her own experiences. Thus, the growth of knowledge is understood in the same way cognitive scientists understand it: as something the child actively constructs through self-motivated actions and experience, not as something we pour into the child from the outside.

We hope our book is useful not only to early childhood teachers, but also to our field, by showing the linkage between the practice of early childhood education and the science of child development. For example, sorting the autumn leaves into different groups, large and small, yellow and red, seems like nothing but a child's game to a naive observer. But this is just the kind of activity that can help children develop their ability to classify into sets, and eventually to cross-classify into multiple sets, which are key mathematical abilities. (See chapter 2.) Similarly, music instruction is fun, and music is a part of a rich life. But it is also more, because children do better on tests of early arithmetic skills when their early care and education programs have more music experiences. (See chapter 3.) These early abilities are important because, as in many areas of children's development, the children who are advanced in their understanding of mathematical concepts in the preschool years tend to remain advanced right through high school.

In the chapters that follow, the main text describes the science of child development, while the inserts and boxes are about the practice of early childhood education. The Promising Practice vignettes in each chapter are real observations from early childhood programs in our home state (Wisconsin). They help illustrate how the concepts from scientific research on child development come to life in the lives of children and their teachers in real programs.

The two types of writing in each chapter, on science and practice, are really just two ways to talk about the same thing. Whatever aspect of child development we are discussing, great professional practice comes from knowing both how children grow (the stages and processes of their development) and what we can do to promote that growth as early childhood teachers. You can read these two parts separately or together, skipping back and forth. The important thing to remember is that the two parts—science and practice—support and enrich each other. The science is meaningless without application in our lives, and the practices can be ineffective when they are not based on the kind of grounded and systemized knowledge provided by science.

The linked fields of child development and early childhood education have much to teach each other. We hope this book is useful in explaining the scientific validity of early care and education practices that look much simpler than they are, and which have much bigger impacts on children's lives than might at first appear.

Why We Chant Nursery Rhymes

The Development of Language and Pre-reading Skills

Ten-month-old Katie holds out her hands toward her caregiver and begins to cry. He looks up from diapering another child and says in a gentle voice, "I see you, Katie. Are you done playing with those rings? I'll be right there." After picking Katie up, he looks in her eyes and asks, "Are you ready for a diaper change, Katie? Let's go over to the diaper table. You can lay down and look at the pictures on the wall while I change your diaper." As he begins to change her diaper, Katie babbles while pointing at one of the pictures. "Do you see the doggie?" her teacher responds. "That doggie is playing in the grass!"

Even during the routine care activity of changing diapers, this early childhood professional is helping to promote Katie's language development. Although he may not be conscious of his actions, research has shown that many of the techniques he uses while talking, listening, and responding to Katie will help her learn to speak and understand language. His skill with Katie is important. He is not only fostering more rapid language development, but also giving this child a head start on schooling and life.

The learning of language is surprisingly similar for children across the world. Regardless of which language they are learning, children develop through the same steps, in the same sequence, at about the same ages. This same sequence and timing is also true for children who are deaf and who are raised in households that use American Sign Language from birth (Newport and Meier 1985). The learning of language is almost certainly one of those universal and unique traits of humans that is inborn and instinctual. But like all our biological inheritances, the success of our unfolding language abilities depends strongly upon our experiences (Shonkoff and Phillips 2000).

In this chapter, we describe the progression of children's language development from birth through age five and explain how specific interactions with caregivers help children to learn these skills. We also describe the skills that toddlers and preschoolers learn that help them become successful readers when they enter school.

Infants

Babies Like to Listen to *Parentese*

From birth, babies listen to adults talking. Newborns look into adults' eyes when they talk to them and may even respond by making sounds of their own.

People generally have a certain way of talking to babies that differs from the way they talk to others. This special kind of talk, which is called *parentese,* is usually spoken more slowly, has a higher pitch, and has more low-to-high and soft-to-loud changes (a singsong quality). Research shows that one-month-olds respond more to parentese than to regular speech directed at adults (Cooper and Aslin 1990). They like it!

Thus, parentese is not just a cute way of talking to babies. It is actually more likely to grab and hold a baby's attention. Parents all over the world use parentese. In fact, even older children use it when talking to a baby. Most of us don't need to be taught to do this; we do it without even noticing. But parentese isn't just "silly talk." This way of talking actually makes some good, scientific sense.

In fact, babies can tell the difference between talk that praises and talk that disapproves. As babies grow, they begin to pay attention to how you sound when talking to them. In one research study, five-month-old babies from English-speaking families listened to audiotapes of parentese in German, Italian, and English (Fernald 1993). Some of the talk praised and encouraged the babies, while other parts of the tape scolded them. The study found that babies smiled when they heard praise in any language, but their faces tensed and they frowned when they heard disapproving words in any language. Even though babies could not see the speaker and didn't understand the language, they were able to recognize the different emotional tones in the words. Thus, from a very early age, children are aware of the social meaning behind adult talk. This is probably why infants are more responsive to parentese and also why this type of talk is beneficial to children.

✓ *Practice Tip*

Talking with Infants

You help infants understand what words mean (their *receptive language* ability) when you talk with them while doing things together such as diapering, feeding, or putting them to sleep.

- Talk so the infant can see your face. Lift the infant up to you or bend down to the infant so your face is directly in front of the infant's face when talking.

- Use *self talk*. Talk about what you are doing with the infant: "I'm putting your diaper in the pail . . . now I'm getting out a clean diaper . . ."

- Describe your actions as the infant watches you: "I'm picking up the toys so we can go for a walk outside."

- Use *parallel talk*. Use words to describe what the infant is doing, seeing, and feeling. "You see the ball on the floor. You want the ball. You're reaching for it. You got the ball!"

- Provide *labels* for things the infant is experiencing. When on a walk, point out and describe the trees, cars, birds, and other things you see on the way.

- *Expand* the infant's understanding by adding more information. "There's a bird. The bird is flying."

Babies Begin to Understand What Words Mean

Even before they can talk, babies begin to understand the meaning of some words (their receptive language ability). This is a simple but important finding. Some adults think talking to babies before they can answer back is silly, but this isn't true. Babies are learning language long before they can speak.

One research study found that babies begin to understand the words "mommy" and "daddy" as early as six months old (Tincoff and Jusczyk 1999). Babies in this study looked more at the picture of their father when they heard the word "daddy" and more at the picture of their mother when they heard "mommy." On the other hand, they did not look more at pictures of men or women who were not their parents when they heard "mommy" or "daddy" being spoken.

By eight months, many infants demonstrate understanding of other commonly used words. In one study, over half of the 1,800 parents in the study reported that their eight-month-olds could understand their own name as well as "mommy," "daddy," "peekaboo," "bye," "bottle," and "no" (Fenson, Dale, Resnick, Bates, Thal, and Petchick 1994). By ten months, children's understanding of words had expanded. Parents reported that over half of the ten-month-olds could understand "all gone," "dog," "uh oh," "ball," "night night," "pat-a-cake," "diaper," "kiss," "book," "yum yum," and "grandma." Keep in mind that the number of words individual children can understand at this age varies. In another study, parents reported that their ten-month-olds could understand an average of about eighteen words, with some parents reporting as few as six or as many as thirty-five words (Bates, Bretherton, and Snyder 1988).

PROMISING PRACTICE

Responding to Cries as Communication

What We Saw

The caregiver plays with an infant on the floor, encouraging him to reach for a toy. The child loses interest and starts to fuss, so the caregiver picks him up, saying, "Maybe you're hungry." She carries him as she checks the notebook for the time of his last feeding. She gets an empty bottle out of the cupboard, asking "Is this what you want?" The infant smiles broadly. The caregiver talks to and holds the baby as she mixes his bottle. "Look at that smile . . . . You are hungry." As she sits with the infant in a rocking chair, she shows him the bottle and waits. She asks, "Want it?" The infant reaches out to hold the bottle, and they settle in for the feeding.

What It Means

The caregiver's sensitive interaction style helps to build the infant's communication skills. She asks the infant what he wants and waits for a response. She is sensitive to his nonverbal cues, and *speaks for the child*, providing the words for the nonverbal response the child gives. The infant is learning that he can communicate his needs to adults by using body movements, facial expressions, and vocalization. When the caregiver correctly reads these messages, the infant does not need to resort to crying.

Babies "Talk" to You Even Before They Say Their First Words

During the first month of life, babies communicate by crying. Anytime they cry, they are trying to tell us something. However, not long after being born, babies learn to make cooing sounds, or long vowel sounds such as "uuuuu." When they are about six to seven months old, they begin to babble consonant and vowel sounds over and over, such as "babababa-ba" (Bee 2000).

When babies are as young as two days old, they often vocalize (make sounds) when people talk to them (Rosenthal 1982). In other words, they "talk" to adults at the same time that adults are talking to them. However, beginning around the age of four months, babies learn that "conversations" require *turn-taking*. That is, when one person is talking, the other remains silent until the person finishes and waits for them to take their turn. Even more surprising, research shows that four-month-olds pause after their mother has finished talking before taking their turn in a "conversation." In fact, just like pauses between turns in adult conversations, the amount of time that babies pause is about the same as the length of pause their mothers wait to speak after their babies have finished vocalizing (Beebe, Alson, Jaffe, Feldstein, and Crown 1988). They make sure it really is their turn, then they "talk" to you. Their language may not be real words, but it is true interaction and communication.

When babies are eight to ten months old, they also begin to use simple gestures, or sign language, to communicate. Over half of the eight-month-olds in one study raised their arms to show that they wanted to be picked up, used gestures to show or give things to others, and smacked their lips to show that something tasted good (Fenson et al. 1994). By ten months, half of the children communicated by pointing, waving, and making requests through gestures. The ability to use gestures signals the onset of *intentional communication* ("talking" with a purpose). This is a key step toward talking.

✔ *Practice Tip*

Beginning Conversations

- Pause and wait for the infant to vocalize (cooing or babbling or even just wiggling) when talking to an infant. If you initially get no response, talk back and wait again for the infant to take a turn.

- Repeat the sound when the infant babbles, to initiate a "conversation," and then talk back, using words to describe the infant's actions or experiences.

- Play turn-taking games such as peekaboo or so big, or even rolling a ball back and forth. Infants love these games because they are predictable. These games teach about cause and effect as well as turn-taking.

- Be sensitive to the infant's responses. When the infant looks away or fusses, it means that it is time to stop.

Table 1.1: Steps in the Development of Language

Age of child	Language skills
Newborn infant	• Communicates primarily by crying • Listens to speech, is especially attentive to *parentese*
1–2 months old	• Laughs and makes cooing vowel sounds, such as "uuuu"
4–5 months old	• Learns to take turns by listening to another speaker and babbling when they pause (*turn-taking* skills) • Recognizes intonation of speech, smiles more when people use a pleasant tone of voice
6–7 months old	• Babbles by using repetitive strings of consonants and vowels, such as "babababababa" • Begins to understand the words "mommy" and "daddy"

7–8 months old	• Begins to understand other common words such as "bye" or "no" (*receptive language*)
8–10 months old	• Uses gestures such as raising their arms or pointing for things, along with sounds, to communicate (*intentional communication*)
12–13 months old	• Understands almost 50 words • Says their first words (*expressive language*)
12–18 months old	• Uses holophrases, by saying one word while also using a gesture to communicate meaning, such as saying "juice" while pointing to the refrigerator to represent the sentence "I want juice."
18–24 months	• Vocabulary spurt begins: Learns to say 10–30 words within a few weeks, most of the words learned are nouns (words for objects) • Says two words together to form a short sentence
27–36 months	• Begins to learn some basic grammar: uses plurals, past tense, verbs such as "is" and "does," and prepositions

BE CONCERNED ABOUT THE INFANT'S LANGUAGE DEVELOPMENT DURING THE FIRST YEAR IF:

- The infant has frequent ear infections or chronic fluid in the middle ear. (The infant may not be hearing sounds or speech clearly.)

- An infant used to babble and then stops making sounds. (The infant may have a hearing impairment.)

- The infant, after eight to ten months, doesn't look when the caregiver points to things. (Joint attention is an important step in communicating.)

- The infant doesn't participate in interactive games such as peekaboo. (The infant hasn't experienced the joy of communicating with others.)

Older Infants Learn to Say Their First Words

Researchers have observed children as young as ten months old beginning to say their first words (Bates, Bretherton, and Snyder 1988). These words include "hi," "bye," and "mama" but also often include sounds that parents understand to represent words, such as an "mmmm" sound that was used by their infants to ask for something. However, most children begin to say their first words when they are about one year old (Fenson et al. 1994).

Learning to say words is called *expressive language*. In one research study, about half of the twelve-month-old children could say "daddy" and "mommy," half of the thirteen-month-old children could say "bye," and over half of the fourteen-month-old children could say "hi," "uh oh," and "dog" (Fernald 1993). "Mommy," "daddy," "dog," and "hi" were also the most common words found among lists of the first ten words said by children in a separate study (Nelson 1973).

Helping Infants' Language Development

Babies Make More Vocalizations When You Play with Them

When you play with babies, they often respond with their own vocalizations (such as babbling or cooing). In one study, researchers observed mothers playing with their babies on their laps every week when the babies were one to six months old (Hsu and Fogel 2001). They found that babies made more sounds (other than crying) when they were more involved with their mothers during play. For example, babies playing a game such as peekaboo with their mothers vocalized more than other babies did. This active communication between mothers and infants also led to more "speech-like" sounds by babies when they were between one and four months old.

Joint Attention Helps Babies Learn Language

Research shows that talking to babies about what they are interested in helps them learn language skills more quickly. When babies and their caregivers are both focused on the same object or activity (called *joint attention*), this turns out to be very important to children's learning. To create joint attention, adults have to pay close attention to what babies are looking at or doing and interpret their meanings or interests.

As children grow older, joint attention can be achieved in other ways. Caregivers may try to direct a baby's attention to a particular toy

☑ *Practice Tip*

Talking to Babies about What They Are Interested In

By eight to ten months, infants have learned to pay attention to the same thing as you and may even be able to direct your attention to something that interests them. This is a crucial step in the development of communication.

- Look at the infant, then at an object while talking about it, to get the infant to look at the object.
- Follow the infant's gaze to an object and talk about what is seen.
- Point to an object and talk about it, encouraging the infant to look.
- Look at books and pictures together, pointing to and talking about what is seen.

These actions help infants make the connection between words and objects.

or activity, even though the baby is looking at something else. This is more difficult for a young child, because it asks him to adapt to you. For example, a caregiver might point to a rabbit in the yard and say "Do you see the rabbit? Can you see her chewing grass?" Caregivers, however, should begin by noticing what babies are already looking at and talk to them about those objects or activities. For example, a teacher might notice that a baby is looking at the mobile hanging above the diaper table and wind the mobile, saying, "Are you looking at the stars up there? Can you see them move?" Researchers find that two-year-olds have larger vocabularies and talk in longer sentences if, back when they were six to eight months old, their parents encouraged joint attention more often with them by directing their attention and by noticing and talking about what the infants were already interested in (Saxon, Colombo, Robinson, and Frick 2000).

PROMISING PRACTICE

Joint Attention

What We Saw

The caregiver sits in a rocking chair with two infants in her lap. Ten-month-old Zack points to a child and makes a sound. Sue responds as if Zack had spoken a name, "Yes, that's Sidney. There's Tyler." Zack points again at Tyler, and Sue says, "Tyler's dancing." He points again and Sue says, "Deb is changing Griffen's diaper." Zack points to a poster on the door and says, "Bi Bir." The caregiver responds, "Yes, that's Big Bird. He has a two on his front. I see Elmo and Ernie and Cookie Monster . . ."

What It Means

Zack has mastered a powerful tool for learning language: pointing. By providing a label or description to what he points to, the caregiver is helping Zack build his *receptive vocabulary* (words he can understand, even though he can't say them yet). Through *joint attention*, Zack has learned that he can communicate with others.

Two more research studies confirm that older infants will learn language more quickly if caregivers talk to them about the activities that have already caught their interest. In one study, children learned to imitate and speak their first words more quickly when their mothers talked to them about what they were doing or about the toys they were playing with when they were nine months old (Tamis-Lemonda, Bornstein, and Baumwell 2001). For example, mothers who were playing with their children might have said, "You're shaking the rattle!" or "That's a doggie," attaching words to the child's own actions. Praising the children's efforts by encouraging them and showing them how to do new things, by saying things such as "Can you move the car like this?" also helped children learn to say their first words more quickly.

You may have noticed that older infants often try to give you their toy when you are sitting near them. Researchers in one study observed eleven-month-olds offering toys to their mothers. The infants had better language skills three months later if mothers responded by talking about the toy (Newland, Roggman, and Boyce 2001). This talk might have included taking the toy and moving it around or telling the child the name of the toy. For example, one mother might have said, "Thank you!" when given the toy. Then she might have continued to talk about the toy by saying, "Look at this kitty. Meow! Meow!" while moving the toy kitten next to her baby.

RESOURCE BOOKS

Among the many excellent resource books that can give you ideas for interactive games to play with infants, here are some we recommend.

Hast, F. and A. Hollyfield. 2001. *More infant and toddler experiences*. Saint Paul, MN: Redleaf Press.

Silberg, J. 2001. *Games to play with babies*. Beltsville, MD: Gryphon House.

Lansky, V. 2001. *Games babies play from birth to twelve months*. Minnetonka, MN: Book Peddlers.

Martin, E. 1988. *Baby games: The joyful guide to child's play from birth to three years*. Philadelphia: Running Press.

Dougherty, D. P. 2001. *How to talk to your baby: A guide to maximizing your child's language and learning skills*. New York: Avery/Penguin Putnam Inc.

☑ *Practice Tip*

Reading Books with Infants

- ◆ Provide cloth or vinyl books the infant can grasp and mouth.
- ◆ Choose books with simple illustrations of familiar objects.
- ◆ Sit with the infant in your lap.
- ◆ Use an expressive voice.
- ◆ Use books as part of a routine, such as before sleep.
- ◆ Label the objects, people, and actions in the book.
- ◆ Read nursery rhymes and poems. Infants are drawn to their lilting rhythms.
- ◆ Stop when the infant loses interest.

Toddlers

Children's Vocabularies Grow Quickly
After They Begin to Talk

Between the ages of eighteen months and two years, most children begin a period of explosive growth in their vocabularies, learning an average of nine new words per day, every day, for the next several years.

Children's first spoken words usually involve either objects that a child can manipulate, such as shoes and balls, or things that move on their own and make their own sounds, trucks, clocks, and different kinds of animals, for example. Children do not begin to talk by learning the names of objects that are motionless, silent, and cannot be moved by the child, such as sofas, tables, and trees, even though these objects are also a part of their daily lives (Nelson 1973). Children seem to focus on objects that move, produce sound, or can be acted upon by the child.

Should We Be Concerned about Late Talking Toddlers?

Research estimates that about 10 to 15 percent of toddlers are late talkers (Rescorla 1989). Two-year-olds with a speaking vocabulary of less than fifty words and who produce no word combinations (two-word or three-word sentences), are considered to be late talkers. These toddlers' expressive language skills (verbal skills) develop more slowly, although they usually have average levels of development in other areas (such as physical skills and intelligence).

Most late-talking toddlers catch up in their vocabulary size within a year or two (Paul 1993). But late talkers may experience other language problems. In one research study, almost two-thirds of children who were late talkers when they were two years old experienced difficulties using correct syntax (word order) at age three, and about half of these children experienced difficulties with articulation (speaking clearly) at age three (Paul 1993). However, fully three-fourths of children who had language delays at age two had no language problems by school age. With no special programs, they grew out of their language delays on their own (Rescorla and Schwartz 1990). On the other hand, just about every five-year-old with a language disability also had a language delay at age two. So, for about one-fourth of children with a language delay at age two, some kind of professional help may be needed.

Can we predict which children will fail to grow out of their language difficulties without help? No, not at present. And we need to be a bit cautious about labeling a child as having a language delay, because excessively worried parents can make children so anxious about their speech that their problems get worse. In very general terms, we should have some concern for two-year-olds who use fewer than fifty words or never use two-word combinations (for example "more milk" or "bye-bye daddy"). These children deserve extra language interaction with their teachers, and if they still lag well behind their peers by age five, professional help is probably needed.

Toddlers Begin to Speak in Sentences and Learn Basic Grammar

When children are first beginning to speak, they may say one word to represent a whole sentence. For example, a child may say "ball" to mean "I want to play with the ball." These one-word "sentences," called *holophrases,* are often accompanied by gestures to help communicate the meaning. Later, when children are closer to two years old, they begin to use simple two-word sentences. (This is true in all languages.) Eventually, these two-word sentences become more complex as children learn how to pluralize nouns (such as from "dog" to "doggies"), use the past tense (such as "talked"), use prepositions (such as "on" or "in"), and use verbs (such as "is" and "does") (Bee 2000).

Promoting Toddlers' Language Development

Secure Attachment to Caregivers Is Associated with Language Development

Children who have secure attachments to their parents also have better receptive (comprehension) and expressive (spoken) language skills when they are two years old (Murray and Yingling 2000). Children who are securely attached to their caregivers (including their fathers and other early childhood caregivers) feel a sense of warmth and safety when their caregivers are nearby. This feeling of safety allows them to try new experiences, because they know they can always return to their caregivers for comfort and support. They have a "safe base" for exploration, so they tend to learn more. Children's emotional development and intellectual development go hand in hand, helping each other develop. Children who are securely attached have caregivers who are *sensitive* to their needs and *responsive* to their attempts to communicate.

✔️ *Practice Tip*

Reading Books with Toddlers

- Provide sturdy board books that can be handled by the child.

- Sit with the toddler in your lap or sitting next to you. Reading individually or to only two or three toddlers at a time works best.

- Use books with simple text and illustrations or photos.

- Focus on talking about the pictures rather than reading the whole book from beginning to end.

- Point to the pictures and describe what is happening.

- Ask the child to point out familiar objects.

- Point to pictures and ask the child to name things.

- Follow the child's interest in the book, letting the child turn pages, go forward and back, open and close, and change books.

- Expect to read favorite books over and over. With a familiar book, you can begin to read a sentence and sometimes the child can finish it for you.

- Stop when the child loses interest.

Toddlers Learn Vocabulary Faster When Their Caregivers Talk to Them More

No surprise: the more parents talk to their children, the more their children's early vocabularies grow (Huttenlocher, Haight, Bryck, Seltzer, and Lyons 1991). In one study, researchers observed children and their parents in their homes every month from the time the children were seven to nine months old until they were three years old (Hart and Risley 1995). They found that children had larger vocabularies at age three when parents spoke more often to them during infancy. In particular, children learned more words by age three when their parents named and described lots of different things to them. Children also learned specific words earlier when they heard their mothers use these words more often. This is especially true for object words. For example, children learned words such as "sock," "desk," or "tree," earlier if their mothers said these words more often.

This makes perfect sense. What is surprising, perhaps, is that some children hear so little of this everyday language. In the above study, one of the toddlers was spoken to by a parent about 56 times per hour, while another was spoken to a whopping 793 times per hour! For children whose families are not talking to them as often, an early childhood program can be crucial to their development, making up for a lack of language stimulation at home.

✔️*Practice Tip*

Talking with Toddlers

- Use words to describe children's feelings and intentions. "You love your teddy bear. You're taking good care of him."

- Insist that the child use words. Some families are so good at understanding a child's gestures that the child doesn't have to really speak. If a child points to the milk and grunts, at some point you may need to pretend that you don't understand. "What is it you want? Can you tell me?"

- Expand the child's one- or two-word speech by restating the complete sentence. "You want to play with the truck."

- Interpret children's actions and intentions to each other. "She wants to play ball with you."

- Provide children with words to use. Say, "Can I have the ball when you are done?"

One of the times during the day when parents differ the most in their language interaction is when doing routine caregiving tasks such as diapering and feeding children. Most people seem to talk with toddlers

☑ *Practice Tip*

Talking about Toys

- ◆ Use nouns and label objects. "Truck. You have a truck."
- ◆ Use adjectives. Describe the color, texture, shape, and sound. "The truck is yellow. The truck goes vroom."
- ◆ Use verbs. Describe what the toy is doing or can do. "You're pushing the truck back and forth."
- ◆ Add information about the object. "It's a dump truck. It can hold sand in the back."
- ◆ Involve the child in exploring the toy. "Fill the truck up with sand."

while playing with them, but some people don't create conversations around the dining table or while diapering. Given the large amount of time spent in routine tasks, this difference matters. In one study, mothers and toddlers were videotaped at home. When mothers talked frequently with lots of different words during routine caregiving tasks, the toddlers were likely to have much larger vocabularies (Hoff-Ginsburg 1991).

The researchers also found that the way parents talked to their children was important. Children had larger vocabularies by age three when they heard their parents talking to them in ways that encouraged them to respond, such as "Do you want some juice?" or "What would you like to play with?" On the other hand, children knew fewer words at age three if their parents used more demands or prohibitions that began with words such as "don't," "stop," and "quit" when talking to their children.

Like most of the research we describe in this chapter, these findings were about parents and their children. Would we find the same thing if we studied early childhood teachers? We believe the influence of parents on children is greatest, but we expect that the same kinds of language behaviors by caregivers would promote children's language development. This idea gains support from a study that examined how the quality of early care and education programs affects children's language development. Researchers found that the amount teachers talked to children predicted children's language abilities when they were one, two, and three years old (NICHD-ECCRN 2000). Specifically, children understood and used more words when they were one-year-olds if their teachers asked them more questions, responded more to their vocalizations, and talked to them in other positive ways. Two-year-olds used more words and said more complex sentences, and three-year-olds knew the names for more objects (verbal IQ) when their teachers talked to them more in these ways. Both current and earlier teacher behaviors predicted children's language abilities at age three.

You might think that the key finding in all this research is the need for early language stimulation, but we think that's not quite right. What young children need is not just language stimulation, but *language interaction*. For example, the language stimulation children receive from TV and radio does little to improve their vocabulary or grammar. This is shown by studies of children who listen to foreign language broadcasts but fail to learn the foreign language. As another example, consider a case study of a four-year-old born to parents who were deaf. They did not speak or sign to him, but he was allowed to watch plenty of television (Sachs, Bard, and Johnson 1981). As a result, he did not talk until he was two-and-a-half years old. When he was almost four, he only talked when asked questions, and when he answered, he used only one- or two-word sentences. His language comprehension could not be measured, because he could not understand the directions for the test. After receiving an intervention from a speech-language therapist that consisted of talking with him about toys and pictures twice per week for one month, his talking increased, he used longer sentences, and he began to learn language rules (such as how to make a noun plural and how to use proper word order). He continued to receive speech-language therapy during kindergarten and first grade.

The language stimulation he had received from television wasn't good enough. What he needed was language interaction (such as joint attention, labeling his actions, and turn-taking conversation).

MISTAKEN PRACTICE

Using Language to Interrupt a Child's Learning

What We Saw

The caregiver sits next to eighteen-month-old Cassie, who has been working on a puzzle. The caregiver says, "You are doing the Sesame Street puzzle." Cassie looks up and smiles, then looks back to the puzzle. The caregiver points to one character after another on the puzzle, naming them, and then begins to ask questions about them. "Look at Elmo. What color is Elmo?" Cassie continues to struggle with the Big Bird piece, which doesn't fit where she has it. The caregiver continues. "Elmo is red. And look, Big Bird is yellow." Cassie continues to work on the Big Bird piece, but then gives up and walks away.

What It Means

Language stimulation is most effective if it focuses on the interests of the child. In this observation, Cassie was most interested in solving the puzzle. The teacher frustrated Cassie by asking a series of *testing* questions about the colors of the pieces. (These are *testing* questions because the teacher already knows the answers.)

What Would Work Better

Provide support by observing the child first, and then if the child appears stuck, say something such as "Big Bird has this long beak. Can you find that same shape on the board? That's where the Big Bird piece will fit."

―――

Dramatic Play Contributes to Toddlers' Language Development

Research shows that children who engage in dramatic play when they are only fourteen months old have better language skills (understand more words and can speak in longer sentences) when they are two years old than children who do not engage in dramatic play (Lyytinen, Laakso, Poikkeus, and Rita 1999). The type of dramatic play makes a difference too. Dramatic play that is social (directed toward others) seems more strongly related to language development than solitary dramatic play. Socially directed play might include brushing a doll's hair or pretending to feed a doll, rather than simply pretending to drink from an empty cup.

Preschoolers

By the time children reach preschool age (three to five years old), they have already passed the major milestones of language development. At this age, children learn to speak even longer sentences as they practice and refine their language skills. They also learn new words even more rapidly than when they were toddlers. The average four- to five-year-old learns five to ten new words per day, every day (Bee 2000). Can you imagine doing this? By the time children are six years old, they are able to recognize an average of more than 10,000 words (Anglin 1993).

Preschoolers Make Interesting Grammatical Mistakes

Preschoolers often make grammatical mistakes, especially when using irregular words. By this age, children have learned how to pluralize nouns by adding an "s" ("tree" becomes "trees") and have learned to use verbs

✅ *Practice Tip*

Reading Books with Preschoolers using Interactive Reading

- Ask questions before and while reading the book about what the book might be about, what might happen next, how characters feel, or what they are doing and why.

- Pause for children to fill in the next word and to join in with repeated phrases.

- Provide actions children can do along with the story.

- Highlight or explain new words.

- Connect books to other classroom activities: read books about gardening when planting seeds, put out books about buildings or vehicles in the block area, or read a book about food before a cooking activity.

- Provide props so children can act out the story afterward.

- Read books to discuss new ideas and experiences, or to explore difficult feelings. Some great preschool books can be found about divorce, new babies, death, and moving to a new town.

in the past tense by adding an "ed" ("play" becomes "played"). Children learn these rules of grammar without ever being taught, which shows how clever they are. However, after learning these rules of grammar, children make mistakes by applying the rules to words that don't follow the usual rules (this is called *over-regularization*). For example, the plural of foot is feet, not foots, and the past tense of eat is ate, not eated, as it should be if the rule were followed. Children start making these mistakes only after becoming familiar with the grammatical rules for regular words.

These mistakes show how smart children really are. They are able to figure out the rules for forming plural and past tense words, and then use those rules to invent words they have never heard spoken, words like foots or eated. They do this even with irregular words that they already know, because when they discover a new rule, they tend to overapply it for a while. This shows that learning language is a lot more than just memorizing and copying what they hear. Young children decode the rules of language, then invent new words according to that code. Their grammar mistakes show us how the English language would be if it followed its own rules, and they show us how smart our children are.

Promoting Preschoolers' Development

Quality Child Care with an Emphasis on Literacy Promotes Language Development

Many studies have found that three- to five-year-old children who attended high-quality early care and education programs had better language skills. In these programs, teachers talk with children more, asking children questions and elaborating on the children's language. (If the child says, "doggie," the teacher might elaborate by saying "He's a big, black doggie.") They also include books, writing materials, and drawing materials that are easily accessible to the children. In addition, a variety of developmentally appropriate activities are available to the children, including art, music, sand and water play, block play, dramatic play, nature or science activities, math and number activities, and fine-motor activities (Dunn, Beach, and Kontos 1994). All of these activities provide preschoolers various opportunities for language interactions, early writing opportunities, as well as exposure to letters and words.

Just as we have seen for infants and toddlers, the environment that preschoolers experience at home is the strongest influence on their language development. But the quality of their early care and education programs is also important. Children with similar family experiences at home have better language skills if they attend higher quality child care (Dunn, Beach, and Kontos 1994; NICHD-ECCRN 2000). And for the children whose home environments provide the least language interaction, a high quality early care and education program can be crucial.

PROMISING PRACTICE

Interactive Book Reading

What We Saw

The preschool teacher reads a book about feelings. As she shows the page, the teacher asks the children to show their silly faces and then their scared faces. During the page on "disappointed," a child asks what that is. The teacher explains, "Like you felt when you couldn't watch your movie yesterday . . . kind of sad and kind of mad." For "thankful," she says, "I'm thankful when you pick up your toys, and . . ." (turning the page to "mad") "I'm mad when you don't." For "frustrated," she talks about "when you can't tie your shoes . . . you get frustrated when you don't get it right." For "excited," she asks, "Were you excited when we climbed over the mountain of snow on our walk?" A boy says, "It was huge." "Huge," the teacher repeats. Another boy adds, "Humungous!" When the teacher reads "scared," one child says, "I'm scared when I'm shy." As she reads about "proud," another child says proudly, "I got dressed by myself."

What It Means

This teacher uses story time as an opportunity to build children's vocabulary as well as their understanding of emotions. She emphasizes the new vocabulary word as she reads and explains the meaning in terms of experiences the children have had. She encourages the children to participate in the discussion by asking questions. Any reading to children is good for their language development, but this style of interactive reading—where you stop and ask questions or discuss the story—has been shown to work especially well.

Involving Children during Shared Book Reading Helps Children Develop Their Language Skills

Research shows that preschool-aged children have better language skills when their child care teachers or parents read to them using a technique called *interactive book reading* (Wasik and Bond 2001; Morrison, Griffith, and Alberts 1997). Instead of just reading the story while children listen, adults ask children to describe the pictures in the book and encourage them to talk about what's happening in the story. This creates a back-and-forth dialogue between children and adults about what's going on in the book while reading. By engaging children's thinking, it promotes their learning.

In one test of interactive reading, three- to four-year-old children who scored lower than average on language tests were divided into four groups (Lonigan and Whitehurst 1998). Children in one group were read to using interactive book reading at home with their parents, and the second group was read to using interactive book reading at their child care program. The third group participated in interactive book reading both at child care and at home. The fourth group of children was read to just as much, but not using this technique. After six weeks, children who participated in interactive book reading, either at home or child care or in both settings, had larger vocabularies, used a greater variety of words, and used more verbs in a storytelling test than children who did not participate in interactive book reading. This really works!

In another study, teacher-caregivers read to four-year-old children, using interactive book reading (Wasik and Bond 2001). They also brought into their classrooms objects for children to play with that were from the books. Finally, they implemented play-center activities related to the themes in the books, providing opportunities for children to use the new words they were learning. For example, two of the books that teachers read were about gardening. So the teachers placed seeds, a shovel, a rake, a watering can, a small version of a garden hose, and flowers in their room. The classroom activities included planting carrot or bean seeds and making a vegetable tray with the children for snack. After fifteen weeks, children who participated in these activities scored better on receptive (comprehension) and expressive (verbal) vocabulary tests using words from the books. They also scored better on a general vocabulary test than children who had not participated in these activities. They also got to eat the carrots and beans they grew!

Second Language Learning

Are Children Confused by Hearing Two Languages in the Home?

We might expect that growing up in a home where two different languages are spoken would be difficult for children who are just beginning to learn language. If we had to guess, we might predict this would delay their learning of language.

Surprisingly, this is not the case. In fact, young children in bilingual households learn both languages at the same time, know when to use one or the other, and accomplish this at very nearly the same pace as children learning a single language (DeHouwer 1995).

The key is living in a truly bilingual world. If they spend much time in a peer group or institutional setting (such as child care or school) that uses just one language, and devalues or forbids the other, then these children can quickly lose much of their early bilingual ability. This is known from research on Mexican American children, which finds a rapid loss of bilingual ability in second- and third-generation children, especially apparent after they reach school age (Hakuta and D'Andrea 1992).

A Bilingual Program Can Maintain Home Language Abilities While Adding English Skills

One research study investigated children's language development in two groups of low-income, Spanish-speaking, Mexican American children (Winsler, Diaz, Espinosa, and Rodriguez 1999). One group attended bilingual early care and education programs for two years. The teacher-caregivers in these classrooms spent approximately half of each day talking to children in Spanish and the other half in English. The second group of children did not attend any type of child care.

After two years, researchers found that children attending the bilingual child care were just as good at understanding and speaking Spanish as children who did not attend child care. But the children who had attended bilingual child care had become far better at speaking English. The children did not lose their Spanish skills, but added English to their abilities.

✓ *Practice Tip*

Extending Literacy Activities to the Home

♦ Prepare "Literacy Bags" for children to take home on a rotating basis, with books, simple games and activities that families can do with their children.

♦ Invite parents in to read a favorite story to the children in your classroom.

♦ Create class books, with each child drawing a picture and dictating a sentence about a trip, a story, or other experience. Bind the pages together into a book for the children to read in the reading corner or to take home on loan (to read to their parents).

♦ Institute a center reading program. Ask parents to keep track of time spent at home reading to their children (or number of books read). This could be a competition with prizes or incentives (books, coupons, or discounts) or a way to promote use of a book-lending library in the program.

Learning Sign Language Is Good for the Language Development of Hearing Children Too

One researcher found that hearing preschool children who learned sign language in an early care and education program showed more improvement in their receptive language skills (understanding the meaning of words) than children who did not learn sign language (Daniels 1994).

In this study, teacher-caregivers in two classrooms included sign language in their daily activities throughout the year, and teacher-caregivers in two other classrooms did not. In the sign language rooms, the teachers at first signed words and phrases while also speaking. Later in the year, they used sign language and English together half of the time, English alone 25 percent of the time, and sign language alone 25 percent of the time. Teachers signed requests, such as "sit," "stop," "stand," "walk," and "line up." They also signed the names of centers and activities in the centers. Children were also taught the signs for the names of letters in the alphabet. Finally, before reading to the children, teachers signed the names of the words that would be introduced in the stories.

Children's receptive language skills were tested at the beginning of the year and at the end of the year. At the beginning of the year, children from the two sign language rooms and children from the non-sign language rooms scored about the same on the test. At the end of the year, the average language scores for children who had learned sign language were significantly higher than the scores of the other children. The children were followed through their kindergarten year, and those who had learned sign language continued to maintain their improved receptive language abilities (even though none of their kindergarten teachers used sign language (Daniels 1996). In some way that we are only beginning to understand, learning sign language is good for the language development of hearing children as well as children who are deaf.

Early Childhood Education Can Add to a Child's Later School Success

Differences between children in language development are huge by the time they reach school age. In one study of five-year-olds entering kindergarten, their receptive vocabularies (understanding the words spoken to them) ranged from the normal vocabulary of a two-year-old (at the low end) to that of an average ten-year-old (at the high end) (Morrison, Griffith, and Alberts 1997). We might expect that school would provide so much language stimulation that children would catch up, but this is not usually the case. Differences at the time of school entry are seldom reduced and often increase with each year of schooling. How well these children succeed in school has already been largely determined before they walk through the door on their first day. If we want to help all children, we must look to their parents and their early care and education teachers.

Many studies have tested whether the quality of child care would influence children's language skills later, when their children entered school. For example, in one study, children from child care programs of differing quality were later tested when they were in kindergarten and second grade (Peisner-Feinberg, Burchinal, Clifford, Culkin, Howes, Kagan, and Yazejian 2001). Programs were considered to be of higher quality if they had more developmentally appropriate play materials and activities, if they were more child-centered, and if teachers were more sensitive and responsive to the needs of children. The researchers tested the children's language abilities by asking them to choose the picture that matched a word. For example, children might have been asked to point to the car among a number of pictures of different things. The researchers found that children who attended higher quality child care centers when they were four years old had better receptive language skills two years later, when they were six years old. High quality early care and education had a positive effect on the language development of children from all backgrounds, but the biggest impact was for children whose mothers had not completed high school.

Song and Rhyme

What We Saw

As the children were getting ready for lunch, a teacher sang "This Old Man," using a puppet with numbered pockets. The children sang along and were eager to find a word that rhymed with each number. One child said that "sign" rhymed with "nine," and the teacher congratulated her on coming up with a different rhyme than the one on the puppet pocket. The girl beamed with pride. Later during lunch, more rhyming words were talked about, such as "cheese" and "please," as well as the rhyming names of two children in the class. Some children noticed that they had some of the same letters in their names that were printed on their place mats.

What It Means

The pacing of music and the rhymes of song are not only fun, but also provide a natural structure for learning language. Pre-reading skills were being reinforced when the children sought words with similar sounds (rhymes) and when they looked at the spelling of their names on their place mats to see if they had some of the same letters.

Learning to Read

Learning early language skills in an early care and education program also improves children's reading abilities when they are older. Another research study found that children from low-income families who attended a full-time, high quality early care and education program from the time they were babies through age five were better readers at age eight and age twenty-one than similar children who did not attend the program (Campbell, Pungello, Miller-Johnson, Burchinal, and Ramey 2001). The high quality program had a low number of children per caregiver, low caregiver turnover, well-trained staff, and a developmentally appropriate curriculum that included playing games with children that helped them

✔ Practice Tip

Rhyming and Alliteration Activities

Nursery Rhymes

One of the reasons for the enduring popularity of nursery rhymes is the effective use of rhyming (ending sounds) and alliteration (beginning sounds). When nursery rhymes are put to music, they can be irresistible.

> *Miss Mary Mack, Mack, Mack,*
> *All dressed in black, black, black,*
> *With silver buttons, buttons, buttons,*
> *Up and down her back, back, back.*

Try singing the beginning of each phrase and letting the children chime in with the repeated words.

Rhyming Songs

> *"Willoughby Wallaby"*
> *"This Old Man"*
> *"The Ants Go Marching"*
> *"Down By the Bay"*
> *"The Name Game"* (Jackie, Jackie, bo backie, banana fana fo fackie, me my mo mackie, Jackie!)

Children's Books with Rhyme and Alliteration

One reason children love these books is that mastering a new skill (in this case phonemic awareness skills) is always very enjoyable. Dr. Seuss's books are famous for their fun rhymes and alliteration.

learn language. For example, in one language game for babies, care-givers called children's names softly when children were lying on their backs, facing away from them (Sparling and Lewis 1979). When children turned their heads toward their voices, caregivers picked the children up and cuddled with them. This language game encouraged babies to listen to language and to learn to use their ears, as well as their eyes, when exploring. Other games were used for toddlers and preschool-age children (Sparling and Lewis 1979; Sparling and Lewis 1984).

Most parents want their children to learn to read, and they are proud when their children memorize the alphabet song. But it turns out that memorizing the alphabet at age three or four doesn't predict that children will be better readers later. What *does* predict reading ability in the elementary school grades are other abilities, especially:

1.   phonological awareness skills

2.   letter name and letter sound skills

3.   learning about print

4.   learning to recognize print within a particular context

Each of these skills will be described in more detail.

1. Phonological Awareness Skills

Phonological awareness skills are the ability to recognize the separate sounds that are used in words, especially:

- *Rhyme:* recognizing words that sound the same in the middle and at the end

- *Alliteration:* recognizing words that sound the same at the beginning

- *Syllable segmentation:* recognizing that words are made up of separate sound units, which are called syllables

- *Phoneme segmentation:* recognizing each individual sound in a word, which is known as a phoneme

Table 1.2: Approximate Ages for Phonemic Awareness Skills (Wasik 2001)

Age of child	Phonological awareness skills	Example
3–4-year-olds	Rhyme	In "Twinkle, Twinkle Little Star," "high" and "sky" rhyme with each other because they end with the same sound.
4–year-olds	Alliteration	The poem "Peter Piper Picked a Peck of Pickled Peppers" illustrates alliteration, since most of the words begin with the same sound, /p/.
4–5-year-olds	Syllable segmentation	The word "chimpanzee" has three syllables: chim-pan-zee. It is easier for younger children to identify the syllables in compound words such as "seashell" and "ballgame" because the syllables are also two separate words: "sea" and "shell," "ball" and "game."
5–6-year-olds	Phoneme segmentation	The word "cat" has 3 phonemes: the /k/ sound, the /a/ sound, and the /t/ sound.

Table 1.2 gives examples of rhyming, alliteration, syllable segmentation, and phoneme segmentation and the approximate age that children begin to learn these skills. Researchers have found that when children learn these skills in preschool, they are better at learning to read words in kindergarten and first grade (Lonigan, Burgess, and Anthony 2000).

Helping preschoolers learn phonological awareness skills not only helps them learn to read words in kindergarten and first grade, but also to read better in the fifth grade. Researchers in a study in Australia randomly assigned preschoolers from four schools into two groups. In the first group, preschoolers were taught to recognize objects that began with the same sound (alliteration) or ended with the same sound (rhyme). This teaching took place for approximately thirty minutes per week for a period of twelve weeks. The control group of preschoolers at each school were instead taught classification skills (such as classifying objects by color). Years later, when these children were in the fifth grade, the children who had been taught to recognize alliteration and rhyme in preschool scored higher on their fifth grade reading tests than the children not taught these skills (Byrne, Fielding-Barnsley, and Ashley 2000).

Many Preschool Activities Help Children Learn to Identify Word Sounds

In another study, four- to five-year-olds in one group experienced rhyme activities during circle time twice per week. These activities included talking about rhymes while seeing pictures and touching objects that rhyme with each other. Another group of four- to five-year-olds was involved in circle time activities that included comparing sizes, locations, shapes, and categories of objects (math activities) instead of talking about rhymes. After only four weeks, children who participated in the rhyme activities at circle time scored better on rhyming-skill tests than children who had not experienced this training (Majsterek, Shorr, and Erion 2000). The activities teachers choose to do with young children really matter.

In another test of preschool activities, four- to five-year-old children participated in activities that focused on five consonant sounds and one vowel sound. One of the consonant sounds was the /s/ sound. To introduce this sound to the children, teacher-caregivers sang songs and recited poems that emphasized the sound to the children during circle time. One example was Shel Silverstein's poem "Sarah Cynthia Sylvia Stout Would Not Take the Garbage Out" because it emphasizes words that begin with the /s/ sound (Silverstein 1974). After talking to the children about how you say the /s/ sound, a poster was brought out that had many objects beginning with the /s/ sound, such as "sea," "seal," "sailor," and "sand." They asked the children to find the objects on the poster that began with the /s/ sound. Later, another poster was used that had many objects *ending* with the /s/ sound, such as "bus," "hippopotamus," "horse," and "octopus." Then children were given pages showing different objects and asked to color the objects that began or ended with the /s/ sound. After these activities had been repeated for the other letter sounds over a period of eleven weeks, cards and games that emphasized these six sounds were brought to the classroom. For example, in a domino game that required children to match different pictures that began or ended with the same sound, a picture of a sun would be placed next to a picture of a sandbox. The researchers found that the children who were exposed to the training for three months got better both at recognizing words that start or end with the six sounds they were trained on and at recognizing other sounds that they were not specifically trained on, as compared with children who did not receive this training (Byrne and Fielding-Barnsley 1991).

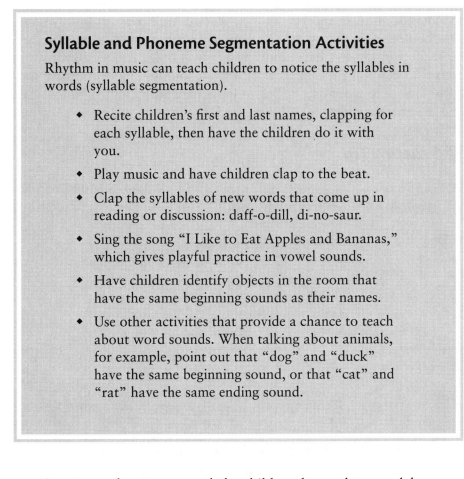

Practice Tip

Syllable and Phoneme Segmentation Activities

Rhythm in music can teach children to notice the syllables in words (syllable segmentation).

- Recite children's first and last names, clapping for each syllable, then have the children do it with you.

- Play music and have children clap to the beat.

- Clap the syllables of new words that come up in reading or discussion: daff-o-dill, di-no-saur.

- Sing the song "I Like to Eat Apples and Bananas," which gives playful practice in vowel sounds.

- Have children identify objects in the room that have the same beginning sounds as their names.

- Use other activities that provide a chance to teach about word sounds. When talking about animals, for example, point out that "dog" and "duck" have the same beginning sound, or that "cat" and "rat" have the same ending sound.

A quieter classroom can help children learn these oral language skills more easily. In one study, children in preschool classrooms in which sound-absorbent paneling was installed scored better on tests of letter, number, and word recognition than the children in the classrooms the year before the paneling was installed. Before the paneling was installed, the classrooms had poor acoustic design because ceilings were high, spaces existed between walls and ceilings, windows and doors were made of glass, and only a small portion of the rooms was carpeted (Maxwell and Evans 2000). This study shows that finding ways to make classrooms quieter could help children hear and recognize letter and word sounds.

2. Letter Name and Letter Sound Skills

Recognizing the names of the letters in the alphabet, and their corresponding sounds, is another key pre-reading skill. Research shows that preschoolers who know letter names and letter sounds become better readers in kindergarten and first grade (Lonigan et al. 2000). Children who develop these skills during preschool will have an easier time "sounding out" words according to letter names and letter sounds when they are ready to begin learning to read.

 *Practice Tip*

Helping Children Learn about Print

- Give children practice in recognizing their names in print. Label children's cubbies, coat hooks, and places at the table with their names. Write their names on their artwork. (If you always write the name on the upper left corner, children will learn that this is where we start to read on a page.)

- Label important things in the room such as activity areas, the sink, tables, and toys on shelves, and include a familiar picture of the item or area labeled, or a symbol with the child's name to help the child "read" the words.

- Make "experience charts" where the teacher writes what children dictate about a field trip, listing children's favorite person, game, or color. You can even write captions on children's drawings as they dictate them to you.

- Point to words on the page as you read them. This helps children relate the spoken word to print, and to isolate and recognize individual words.

- Include a center in your classroom that is only used for children's writing. This center should have a visible alphabet that children can use when attempting to write letters and words, as well as word cards with pictures of common objects such as vehicles, fruit, and various shapes. The center should also have letter stencils and stamps for children to use, as well as a variety of writing utensils and paper (lined, unlined, construction) for children to use.

- Include an accessible listening center that children can use with minimal teacher assistance (or independently if appropriate for the children in your class) so that children can listen to stories while looking at the corresponding books.

- Orient your wall displays so they always run from left to right and top to bottom, the same way a printed page works. This includes displays such as calendar months or days. Your poster of the daily schedule can include picture graphics to represent each activity on the schedule.

- Create charts of favorite stories or songs using titles and picture graphics so that children can make choices during circle time. Take photos of class activities and events and post them around the room with names and captions.

- Include puzzles that display the alphabet, as well as pictures that are labeled; for example, an apple, a bird, or a truck.

- Create a system where children move name tags to indicate which area of the room they will play in.

- Provide rebus stories where some words are replaced with picture symbols for children to participate in reading.

- Take children on "reading walks" in the neighborhood. Help them notice street signs and store signs so they can see themselves as readers. Talk about the usefulness of being able to read these signs to get where they want to go.

3. Learning about Print

Another important skill is learning how print works. For example, children begin to learn that printed words are read and the surrounding pictures are not. They also learn that print is read from left to right and from top to bottom. Learning about the conventions of print helps children develop the skills that lead to later reading. Research shows that children ages three to six who know more about print conventions are also more likely to be able to recognize the correct orientation of a particular letter in the alphabet. For example, children who know about print will spot a backward "B" and know that it is wrong. They are also more likely to recognize that one word is different from another, because its letters are different. Children who have learned more about print are more likely to recognize letter names and sounds (Lomax and McGee 1987).

4. Learning to Recognize Print within a Particular Context

Finally, children learn to read words more easily when familiar pictures surround the words. These pictures or graphics are known as the *environmental context* of the word. In one study, four- and five-year-olds who were able to read a word accompanied by its familiar graphics were also more likely to be able to read the word when its familiar graphics were not present. For example, children who could read the word "McDonald's" when the golden arches surrounded the word were also more likely to be able to read the word "McDonald's" without the familiar golden arches. They were not as likely to be able to read a word that they had never seen with any familiar graphics, such as the word "monster" (Cronin, Farrell, and Delaney 1999). This study provides support for the common practice of labeling items, areas, and centers in preschool classrooms, because children seem to learn how to read these words faster if they are seen daily next to familiar pictures or graphics.

Conclusion

From the moment they are born, children begin to learn about language. Children's language skills progress from listening to and gradually understanding what words mean, to learning to talk, by first saying a few words and later learning to speak in complex sentences. These early oral language skills, which have always been a part of good early childhood programs, lay the foundation for later skill at reading and writing. In fact, much of children's ability to succeed in their later schooling is already determined before their first day of kindergarten. Great early childhood programs can make all the difference for children's later success, especially for children whose families are not able to provide the richness of language interaction that each child needs.

Further Reading

On Research

Adams, M. J., R. Treiman, and M. Pressley. 1998. Reading, writing, and literacy. In *Handbook of child psychology, Vol. 4. Child psychology in practice*, Eds. I. Sigel and A. Renninger, 275–355. New York: John Wiley & Sons.

Armbruster, B. B., and C. R. Adler. 2001. *Put reading first: The research building blocks for teaching children to read*. This and other useful publications are available free on the Web site of the National Institute for Literacy at http://www.nifl.gov/.

Baghban, M. 2007. Scribbles, labels, and stories: The role of drawing in the development of writing. *Young Children* 62 (1): 20–26.

International Reading Association. 2005. Literacy development in the preschool years. Newark, DE at http://www.reading.org/resources/issues/positions_preschool.html.

Mayer, K. 2007. Research in review: Emerging knowledge about emergent writing. *Young Children* 62 (1): 34–40.

The Center for Early Literacy Learning at http://www.earlyliteracylearning.org/index.php.

On Practice

Bobys, A. R. 2000. What does emerging literacy look like? *Young Children* 55 (4): 16–22.

Bowman, B., ed. 2002. *Love to read: Essays in developing and enhancing early literacy skills of African American children*. Washington D.C.: National Black Child Development Institute.

Fowler, W. 1995. Language interaction techniques for stimulating the development of at risk children in infant and preschool day care. *Early Child Development and Care* 111:35–48.

Hohmann, M. 2002. *Fee, fie, phonemic awareness: 130 pre-reading exercises for preschoolers*. Ypsilanti, MI: High-Scope Press.

Jalongo, M. R. 2004. *Young children and picture books*. Washington D.C.: National Association for the Education of Young Children.

Kratcoski, A. M., and K. B. Katz. 1998. Conversing with young language learners in the classroom. *Young Children* 53 (3): 30–33.

Neuman, S. B., C. Copple, and S. Bredekamp. 2000. *Learning to read and write: Developmentally appropriate practices for young children.* Washington, D.C.: National Association for the Education of Young Children.

Owocki, G. 2001. *Make way for literacy: Teaching the way children learn.* Fort Worth, TX: Heinemann Books and Washington, D.C.: National Association for the Education of Young Children.

Rosemary, C. A., and M. P. Abouzeid. 2002. Developing literacy concepts in young children: An instructional framework to guide early literacy teaching. *Journal of Early Childhood Education* 23:181–201.

Roskos, K. A., J. F. Christie, and D. J. Richgels. 2003. The essentials of early literacy instruction. *Young Children* 58 (2): 52–60.

Schickedanz, J. A., and R. M. Casbergue. 2004. *Writing in preschool: Learning to orchestrate meaning and marks.* Newark, DE: International Reading Association.

Selman, R. C. 2001. Talk time: Programming communicative interaction into the toddler day. *Young Children* 56 (3): 15–18.

Vestergaard, H. 2005. *Weaving the literacy web: Creating curriculum based on books children love.* Saint Paul, MN: Redleaf Press.

Wasik, B. A. 2001. Phonemic awareness and young children. *Childhood Education*, Spring, 128–133.

Children's Books

Alphabet Books

Aylesworth, J. 1992. *Old black fly.* New York: Henry Holt and Co.

Base, G. 1987. *Animalia.* New York: H.N. Abrams.

Bayer, J. 1984. *A, my name is Alice.* New York: Dial Books for Young Readers.

Brown, M. W. 1953. *Sleepy abc.* New York: Lothrop, Lee, and Shepard Co.

Carle, E. 1967. *The say-with-me abc book.* New York: Holt, Rinehart, and Winston, Inc.

Carlson, N. 1997. *ABC, I like me!* New York: Viking.

Christensen, B. 1994. *An edible alphabet.* New York: Dial Books for Young Readers.

Demi. 1985. Demi's *Find the animal abc.* New York: Putnam.

Ehlert, L. 1989. *Eating the alphabet: Fruits and vegetables from a to z.* New York: Harcourt Brace Jovanovich.

Eichenberg, F. 1952. *Ape in a cape: An alphabet of odd animals.* New York: Harcourt Brace.

Kirk, D. 1998. *Miss Spider's abc.* New York: Scholastic.

MacDonald, S. 1986. *Alphabatics.* New York: Bradbury Press.

Martin Jr., B., and J. Archambault. 1989. *Chicka chicka boom boom.* New York: Simon & Schuster.

Owoo, I. 1991. *A is for Africa.* Trenton, NJ: Africa World Press.

Seuss, Dr. 1963. *Dr. Seuss's abc.* New York: Random House.

Tudor, T. 1954. *A is for Annabelle.* New York: Oxford University Press.

Updike, J. 1995. *A helpful alphabet of friendly objects.* New York: Alfred A. Knopf.

Van Allsburg, C. 1987. *The z was zapped: A play in twenty-six acts.* Boston: Houghton Mifflin.

Rhyming and Alliteration Books

Ahlberg, J., and A. Ahlberg. 1978. *Each peach pear plum.* New York: Viking.

Buckley, H. E. 1999. *Where did Josie go?* New York: Lothrop, Lee, and Shepard.

Calmenson, S. 1998. *The teeny tiny teacher.* New York: Scholastic.

Cole, J., and S. Calmenson. 1996. *Bug in a rug: Reading fun for just beginners.* New York: Morrow Junior Books.

Cullen, C. A. 2001. *The magical, mystical, marvelous coat.* Boston: Little, Brown and Co.

Denton, K. M. 1998. *A child's treasury of nursery rhymes.* New York: Kingfisher.

Heller, N. 1999. *Ogres! ogres! ogres!: A feasting frenzy from a to z.* New York: Greenwillow Books.

Jonas, A. 1997. *Watch William walk.* New York: Greenwillow Books.

Martin, B. 1967. *Brown bear, brown bear, what do you see?* New York: Henry Holt and Co.

Mosel, A. 1968. *Tikki tikki tembo.* New York: Holt, Rinehart and Winston.

Opie, I. 1996. *My very first Mother Goose*. Cambridge, MA: Candlewick Press.

Prelutsky, J. 1986. *Read-aloud rhymes for the very young*. New York: Alfred A. Knopf.

Root, P. 1998. *One duck stuck*. Cambridge, MA: Candlewick Press.

Sendak, M. 1972. *Chicken soup with rice: A book of months*. New York: HarperCollins.

Seuss, Dr. 1960. *One fish, two fish, red fish, blue fish*. New York: Random House.

Seuss, Dr. 1963. *Hop on pop*. New York: Random House.

Seuss, Dr. 1965. *Fox in socks*. New York: Random House.

Willard, N. 1991. *Pish posh said Hieronymus Bosch*. San Diego: Harcourt Brace Jovanovich.

When Teachers Reflect

1. Not all cultures or families promote language learning in the same way. In some cultures, children are encouraged to be quiet, and the focus is on nonverbal communication between parent and child. Children are always present during adult activities, absorbing language indirectly while listening to adult conversations. Would a child who is used to this indirect language have difficulty responding to a more direct style of communication in your classroom? What challenges might arise from this different caregiving approach? How can you respect the family's culture while also promoting the child's language development?

2. What about children whose families speak a language other than English? How can you support a child in becoming bilingual without undermining the child's connection to the family and home culture? Think especially about this: what are the things we might do *because* we are trying to help the child grow (with the best of intentions), but which could have the unintended side effect of being offensive to the parents' culture?

3. If a quiet classroom environment improves children's early language and literacy skills, what happens in a classroom where loud music is always playing during children's free playtime? Does the music interfere with children's ability to hear phonemes in words? Does music hurt other pre-reading skills and practice? How could carefully selected music help children's language development?

4. How do the adults in the classroom talk with the children? Try listening to your own conversations with children, or observe in another classroom to listen to the children and teachers. (You could use a tape recorder, which makes it easier to really listen.)

   • Does the teacher have a friendly tone, or sound impatient or rushed?

- Whose voice are you hearing the most, adults' voices or children's voices?

- What is the teacher saying? Does the teacher mostly give directions, ask questions, direct behavior, or encourage conversation?

- Does the teacher ask mostly yes/no questions or questions that invite longer answers?

- Does the teacher ask *testing* questions (to which the teacher knows the right answer) or questions that are genuine (to which the teacher does not know the answer)? Can you think of questions you could ask of children that they know the answer to, but you don't?

- After talking, does the teacher pause to wait for the child to respond (especially important with infants and toddlers)?

5. During and after your next free-choice time, think about your conversations with the children, as well as the environment that you created for them. How much did you actually talk with the children? Did you spend more time talking to them or attending to classroom management tasks? Were your conversations with children mostly about things such as directives, behavioral issues, and yes/no questions, or did you attempt to engage children in rich conversations—expanding vocabulary, as well as asking children to elaborate on their activities and discoveries? At the same, did situations occur where you may have "overwhelmed" a child with questions that may have actually led to him becoming disinterested? Finally, how do you think the classroom environment and activities influenced children's language development opportunities? For example, were learning centers available that encouraged conversations between peers? Did you provide an art activity that prompted children to talk about their creations?

Letter to Parents

Children's Language Development Starts Early

Did You Know?

Even before she can speak, your baby is learning language. The more you talk with your baby in the first two years of life, the more words she will know as a toddler and preschooler.

Things You Can Do

Talk about what you are doing as you care for your baby. "I'm going to pick you up and change your diaper now."

Talk about what your baby is seeing, hearing, and doing. Talk about his reactions to those experiences. "See the teddy bear? He's soft and brown. You want to hold the teddy bear. You like him!"

Did You Know?

Cuddling and playing with your baby will help him learn to speak. A nurturing bond between baby and parent, and a home rich in things to play with, helps him learn to understand and communicate.

Things You Can Do

Respond to your baby's cries. Tell her that you love her and are there to take care of her. Play little games such as so big and peekaboo. Provide interesting things for her to look at, touch, and explore. Talk to her about these things. Play together!

Did You Know?

All children make mistakes when learning to talk. "I drawed you a picture." These mistakes show that your child is learning the rules of language (imperfectly at first).

From *Intellectual Development: Connecting Science and Practice in Early Childhood Settings* (Redleaf Press, 2009).

Things You Can Do

Rather than correcting his incorrect words, just accept them for now. Avoid discouraging him from talking. You can restate the message using the correct words or grammar: "You drew me a picture? It's beautiful. Thank you!" He will correct his own grammar by listening to you.

From *Intellectual Development: Connecting Science and Practice in Early Childhood Settings* (Redleaf Press, 2009).

Why We Count While Jumping

The Development of Early Mathematical and Logical Thinking

> *Heidi, the teacher, notices that Damon and Jack are anxious to help her pack the lunch for their picnic at the park. "Let's see," she says. "How many paper plates and cups do we need to take?" She points to the names on the bulletin board and asks, "How many children are here today?" Damon touches each name as he counts the number. "Eight!" he shouts. "Okay," Heidi says, "We also need plates and cups for the teachers. So, if we have eight children and two teachers, how many plates do we need?" She looks to Jack while holding up her fingers for him to count. He counts her fingers and shouts out, "Ten!" with a smile. "You're right! Jack, you can count out ten plates, and Damon you can count out ten cups and put them in our picnic basket."*

Like Damon and Jack, most young children are proud and eager to demonstrate their knowledge of numbers. Creative early childhood teachers like Heidi can find opportunities throughout the day for children to learn about numbers and other mathematical concepts. Heidi is very skilled at this. With her prodding, the two boys work on the logic of one-to-one correspondence (a name for each number, and one cup for each plate) and simple addition. These are some of the early building blocks of mathematical thinking.

Many scholars believe that humans have an inborn ability to learn mathematics. In the same way that children around the world go through a remarkably similar sequence and timing of steps in learning their native language, children also look very similar in their development of logical and mathematical reasoning skills. And as with language, the amount and kinds of experiences young children have with number concepts makes a big difference in how well they learn. In fact, researchers have found a relationship between children's prekindergarten math abilities and their tenth-grade math achievement (Stevenson and Neuman 1986).

LEARNING MATH CONCEPTS THROUGH SONGS AND RHYMES

Old nursery rhymes have helped many children to count, and they still work with today's children. "Baa, baa, black sheep," is a favorite of toddlers, who are just learning to count to three. It is an early reinforcement of one-to-one correspondence.

Baa, baa, black sheep have you any wool?
Yes sir, yes sir, three bags full.
One for my master and one for the dame,
And one for the little boy who lives down the lane.

Another favorite of preschoolers is "One, two, buckle my shoe." Buckles are almost gone on today's shoes, but children like the sound of the word and will mimic a buckle closing once the teacher demonstrates it. The actions can be pantomimed, or the teacher could allow a child to shut the door, pick up sticks, and so forth. Older children can be challenged to change the ending rhyming words to something different to change the routine.

One, two, buckle my shoe.
Three, four shut the door.
Five, six pick up sticks.
Seven, eight lay them straight.
Nine, ten do it again.

Early Mathematical Development

Even newborns have some math abilities. Infants only a few days old can tell the difference between two and three objects (Antell and Keating 1983). You might wonder how researchers can know this. They use a habituation procedure to test newborns' ability to distinguish between different sets of objects.

✔ *Practice Tip*

Teaching Children to Classify into Categories

Try playing the classification game with toddlers. Pour out a pile of objects (such as blocks of different sizes, shapes, and colors) and ask the child to "put together things that are alike." Then simply watch what the child does, describe it aloud to the child, and ask questions about why objects are in one pile or another. Don't expect children to consistently form classes of objects very well until age four or five.

Try sorting buttons into different jars or a sorting tray. Also, try using tongs, tweezers, a spoon, or chopsticks for picking up the buttons or blocks.

Be prepared to ask four- or five-year-olds who are sorting what they are using as the category. They might be using a characteristic you did not notice. "I put together all the beads that sparkle." Time is essential in building the ability to classify. Children must have playing time to explore different groupings of objects, and to develop more sophisticated and complex categories.

Simplify Classification

You can make the initial learning of classification easier by providing materials that differ in only one way. For example, provide only red circles and squares that are all the same size, when asking a child to sort them into separate piles. Since only the shape is different, the child will be more likely to focus on that one characteristic when grouping them. Or you can provide a stronger visual clue to support consistent classification—all the circles are red and all the squares are green. Color then becomes an added clue for sorting.

Infants were shown cards with a small number of black dots on them, sometimes changing the number of dots or the space between them. Infants showed they had "habituated" to the cards (the cards had stopped being new and interesting) when they began to look at them for a shorter amount of time. Like the rest of us, infants are less interested in something that has grown familiar. After they had habituated to a card, a new card with a different number of dots was shown. If the newborns looked at the new card for a longer period of time, this showed they viewed it as different. Based on the infants' reactions to the cards, the researchers inferred that the newborns understood the difference between "two" and "three."

Some researchers believe these findings mean that infants have an early understanding of numbers (Starkey and Cooper 1980), but most now believe that babies are simply aware of greater and lesser amounts of things, not the actual number (Mix, Huttenlocher, and Levine 2002).

Classifying Objects into Categories

Babies come equipped to understand "more" and "less." Toddlers build from these skills and begin to invent ideas about "same" or "different." This is the ability to form classes of objects, a very important concept in mathematics and logic.

Toddlers can classify objects, but not very consistently. Give a toddler a pile of blocks of different colors and shapes and ask her to group things that go together. She may put a blue square and a blue circle together, which is good: they share the same color. (The child is classifying objects by color.) But then next to the blue circle the child might place a red circle. Now the child has shifted from using color to using shape. Because the thinking of toddlers is so dependent upon the physical appearance of the objects they currently see, they rapidly shift categories, forgetting any "classification rule" they may have adopted, such as the color blue.

As their classification skills continue to develop, toddlers begin to classify objects in a more consistent manner, but still have difficulty coordinating one classification rule with another. For example, a toddler may tell you that a blue circle and a blue square are the same (color) or different (shape), but cannot yet see them as both the same and different. They have to be either one or the other. The toddler cannot yet hold two ideas (in this case, two different ways to classify objects) in mind at the same time and coordinate them.

Between the ages of four and seven, children begin using two classifications at once. For example, you can put two hoops on the rug so they overlap and tell the child that blue blocks go in the first hoop, and square blocks go in the second hoop. At some point, a very excited preschooler will discover that blue squares should go into both hoops, which is the area where the hoops overlap. Similarly, at age five or older you can give a child a set of blocks in two shapes and two colors, and instead of just sorting them into two piles (by either shape or color), a very excited child may discover the idea of a two-by-two classification by both shape and color into four piles. This discovery by the child represents the triumph of logic over mere appearances.

LEARNING SHAPES AND PATTERNS WITH PATTERN BLOCKS

A standard set of pattern blocks, available from a store or toy-lending library, has about 250 pieces in six standard shapes (such as square, triangle, trapezoid, and hexagon). Each block has one-inch sides so they fit together neatly, and some shapes can be combined to form the exact shape of other blocks. (For example, two of the green triangles will fit exactly on top of a single blue parallelogram.)

Children (and adults) love to play with these blocks. While experimenting with surprising and beautiful designs or repeating patterns, children can learn shape names, part-whole relations, and symmetry.

Besides free play, you can also challenge children's thinking with pattern block puzzles. Buy or make your own pattern frames that children can try to solve. The pattern is an open area that does not have blocks drawn on it, and the child's task is to find a combination of blocks that fill it completely. With toddlers, draw the blocks inside the frame to make it easy. With preschoolers, leave the open area open. Then the preschoolers may make the interesting discovery that there are usually many solutions to each pattern. This discovery leads to another: that certain combinations of shapes form equivalencies with others. (One can be substituted for the other at any time.)

A pattern frame can be cut from wood, cardboard, or foam board, or even just drawn on a sheet of paper.

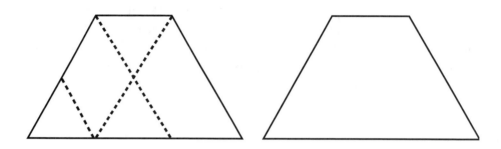

Frames for pattern blocks, with the blocks drawn on the inside (for toddlers) or left open (for preschoolers)

Learning to Identify Common Shapes

Three- to five-year-olds are just beginning to recognize the differences between different geometric shapes. One research study found that children learn how to correctly identify circles first, possibly because circles can only differ in size, not in orientation (Clements and Sarama 2000). By three years old, most children could tell the difference between circles and other shapes, although children three to five years old sometimes mistakenly labeled ellipses as circles.

Squares are the next shape that preschoolers are able to identify. In learning to identify squares, the most common mistake is to label all four-sided shapes as squares, not being able to distinguish a rectangle from a rhombus (which has four sides of unequal length). This is similar to the way preschoolers organize their early language concepts. At first, they may use the word "dog" to mean any kind of four-legged animal, and then with experience, preschoolers develop the idea and words to describe different subtypes of four-legged animals: dogs, cats, cows, and so forth.

Triangles and rectangles are more difficult shapes for preschoolers to identify. Three-year-olds often choose any shapes with points when asked to choose triangles. Older preschoolers also tend to reject triangles that are in different orientations or have different side lengths than the common equilateral triangle (a triangle with sides of equal length). Children are still learning the characteristics of this category called "triangle"—any shape with three straight sides.

LEARNING SPATIAL RELATIONSHIPS

Older preschoolers can enjoy the game of trying to make a simple block construction (one to five blocks) from a card that has the top, front, and side view of the construction. Tangrams are an ancient and fun form of this. They have cards with outlines of things (for example, a house or a boat), and the child must place the seven differently shaped tiles on the card to match the outline.

Building bigger block structures such as a house or a truck provides many opportunities for young children to think and reason about spatial relations. This kind of involved activity also offers many opportunities for teachers to extend children's learning through questions and comments.

Recognizing Differences Between Small Sets of Objects Based on Number

By the time children are two-and-a-half years old, most can use number rather than amount to compare two small sets of objects. This process of recognizing the number of objects in a set without counting is called *subitizing*. (You do this too: when four birds fly overhead, you don't have to count to know there are four.)

For example, in one research study, two-and-a-half- to five-year-olds were shown an array of poker chips and were then briefly shown small dots of light on a screen (Starkey and Cooper 1995). They were asked whether the dots and the poker chips were the same or different in number. The two-and-a-half-year-olds were able to correctly compare the objects based on number if there were one to three objects present in one of the sets. By three-and-a-half years old, children were able to distinguish differences for up to four objects.

When the researchers looked at the mistakes children made for larger numbers of objects, they found that children used length of the line of dots, rather than number of dots, when the number of objects was too large for children to subitize. Children assumed that the longer the line, the more objects it contained. Like classifying objects, young children's thinking about number is at first dominated by the visual appearance of things more than by logic.

LEARNING MATH FROM GOLDILOCKS

The story of Goldilocks is a math lesson about size relationships. The mother bear's bowl was smaller than papa bear's,
but larger than baby bear's. One reason that young children
love the story is that they are wrestling to understand this very
issue—relative size differences—in their logical thinking during the preschool years.

✓ Practice Tip

Simplifying Counting

To facilitate children's accurate counting of objects, place them
in a row (at first) rather than in a random arrangement. Having
a clear place to begin and end the counting sequence promotes
consistent application of one-to-one correspondence.

When working with larger numbers of objects, place them
in groupings of two to three objects to enable visual recognition of quantity (subitizing). For example, placing nine counting
bears in three groups of three enables the child to recognize the
pattern of three. ("Three groups of three bears is nine bears.")
This also is a physical representation of $3 \times 3 = 9$, helping
children gain an intuitive understanding of multiplication long
before they will begin to learn it conceptually.

Understanding "Number" Differently Than Adults

Children as young as two can sometimes count from one to twenty, but
it is unlikely they understand the concept of number yet. This is like
children who can recite the alphabet song, but cannot identify a letter or
its sound. In both cases, they have memorized a sequence, without understanding its meaning. (Similarly, a parrot might memorize and repeat
a series of sounds without understanding their meaning.)

How can you tell this is true? Ask a child to divide a pile of about
twenty pennies into two piles that have the same number. Most two- and
three-year-olds will make two piles that look about equal, but often do
not have exactly the same number. If you ask a three-year-old how she

knows the two piles have the same number, she will simply look at them again to check how they look. Most three-year-olds still are limited to visual appearance in making an estimate of equal amounts, because they have not yet developed our adult understanding about the meaning of number.

Here is something you can try with preschoolers. Lay out two lines of ten poker chips (or buttons or pennies). If each line is the same length, three-year-olds will tell you that each line has the same number. But if you then stretch out one of the lines so it is longer (even while the child watches), the typical three-year-old insists that the longer line now has more chips.

The child's judgment, in this case, is dominated by physical appearances (the line is longer) rather than by an understanding of underlying realities (number). Children this age lack much of the mathematical logic we take for granted. In this case, the child lacks:

- *One-to-one correspondence:* each chip corresponds to a single chip in the other line, so they must have the same number.

- *Conservation of quantity:* if you didn't add or take away any chips, then you must still have the same amount.

Most adults believe they've always known these principles because they seem so obvious. However, children must develop these ideas through experiences with materials and interactions with adults.

LEARNING ONE-TO-ONE CORRESPONDENCE

Any time you encourage children to count while they are doing an activity, their actions will help them learn the concept of one-to-one correspondence (one number matched to one action). Have children count while they jump and count while they swing. Make a rule: ten swings on the swing, then it is someone else's turn. Everyone will count aloud.

Music time is great for learning one-to-one correspondence. Play a short rhythm of a few beats on a drum for the children to repeat. Musicians refer to this as "call and response." As the children get better, your "call" can become more complex. The children are creating a one-to-one match to your rhythm. Vary the rhythm and ask children to match (short-short-long-short-short-long). This is patterning. Of course, let the children take turns going first, too, and you give the response.

A similar game of call and response can be played with blocks. Take a few blocks and make a simple construction with them, then let a child try to copy it exactly with another set of blocks. These are concrete actions that represent one-to-one correspondence. Children can really enjoy these games, because they are exercising the capabilities they are currently working to develop.

When children are between three and four years old, they begin to develop the ability to more accurately compare the sizes of numbers. For example, in one research study, children watched while two stuffed animals were given a certain number of grapes or marbles. Children were then asked which animal received more. Researchers found that three-year-olds understood the differences between small numbers (one to four) and large numbers (five to nine), but they could not understand differences in number magnitude within these categories. For example, they did not know which animal had more if one had five grapes and the other had six grapes. Four-year-olds, on the other hand, could understand the differences between small (one to three), medium (four to six), and large

✔ Practice Tip

Demonstrating Large Numbers Concretely

Children have a difficult time understanding the meaning of larger numbers. You can help them understand and learn about numbers by providing a concrete demonstration of number sizes. For example, show them with a measuring tape how old the four-year-olds are: four inches. Now show them how old you are with the same measuring tape! You can also use the measuring tape to give children an appreciation of time, such as number of days until a holiday or number of years since your town was settled.

Some preschool programs celebrate the hundredth day of school. In some classrooms, children make a loop in a chain for each day, or add a marble to a jar, or a mark to a chart. In one classroom, children were asked to bring in a hundred objects. They varied from pennies to stickers to cotton swabs. This is a fun way to demonstrate large quantities.

(seven to nine) numbers. They could also distinguish differences within the small category. They understood that one is smaller than two, two is smaller than three, and three is smaller than four. They could not distinguish these same types of differences within the medium or large categories. (For example, they couldn't tell the difference between five and six, or seven and eight.)

Learning to Count

On average, three-year-olds can count to twelve, and four-year-olds can often count to forty (Murray and Mayer 1988). How do children learn to do this? Besides learning number words, preschoolers need to understand three principles before they understand the idea of numbers well enough to accurately count:

- one-to-one correspondence,
- stable order (sometimes called "ordinality"), and
- cardinality (Gelman and Gallistel 1978).

See Table 2.1 for a brief explanation and example of each principle.

Table 2.1: The Three Counting Principles (Gelman and Gallistel 1978)

Counting principle	Explanation	Example
One-to-one correspondence principle	Each object should be labeled with only one number, so that no object is missed and the same object is not counted twice.	If counting two trucks, the red truck is labeled "1" and the blue truck is labeled "2." The red truck cannot be relabeled "3."
Stable order principle	The same sequence of numbers must be used to label objects each time they are counted.	If counting four blocks, the number sequence must be "1, 2, 3, 4," *not* "1, 4, 3, 2," *or* "1, 2, 5, 6."
Cardinality principle	The number that is said last represents the number of objects that have been counted.	When counting out plates for lunch, you have ten plates when you end with the number "10."

Three- to four-year-olds are just beginning to learn these three counting principles. Even though children often make mistakes when counting at this age, research shows that children often can identify another person's counting errors. For example, one research study examined whether children would be able to catch a puppet's counting mistakes when the puppet violated one of these principles (Gelman and Meck 1983).

Most three- and four-year-olds were able catch the puppet's violation of *the one-to-one correspondence principle*. That is, when the puppet skipped one of the objects or counted one of the objects twice, most children said that the puppet's counting was wrong. (Try this and the other mistakes with a puppet at circle time. Children love to catch you or the puppet making a mistake, and they will learn from each other!)

Most three-, four-, and five-year-olds also said the puppet's counting was wrong if the puppet reversed the order of two numbers when counting or used a random sequence of numbers when counting, both violations of *the stable order principle*. However, three-year-olds seldom caught the puppet skipping numbers when counting (for example, "one, two, five, six") Skipping numbers is a common counting mistake among three-year-olds.

Finally, almost all of the three- and four-year-olds knew when a puppet's final answer of the number of objects that had been counted was right or wrong. When the puppet violated *the cardinality principle* by stating that the number was one more (or less) than had been counted, children almost always said the puppet's answer was wrong. So, by three to four years old, children are learning the counting principles, even though they may continue to make counting mistakes (especially when counting larger numbers of objects).

PROMISING PRACTICE

Linking Numbers to Personal Experience

What We Saw

The classroom keeps a thermometer outside. At circle time every day, the teacher brings it in and discusses the temperature with the children. "The thermometer says it's twenty-five degrees. That's cold! Can you feel how cold that is?" She passes the metal thermometer to the children. She brings down a chart that records the week's temperatures. "On our chart, can you show me where twenty-five degrees is?" One child points to a number. "You are going too high," she suggests. "Yesterday it was warmer, remember? Here is the bar for yesterday. Today it is colder, so the number for our temperature is smaller." She helps a child to select the number twenty-five, and she draws a line across the bar graph at that point. One of the children then colors in the bar.

What It Means

Children need lots of experience before they understand that numbers represent quantities and that most things in their world can be measured with numbers. Here the teacher connects the children's own experience (of temperature) to numbers. Having the children help produce the bar chart is a great idea: they can begin to visually compare quantities from one day to the next. Because bigger numbers have longer bars on the chart, the bar chart teaches that larger numbers represent larger quantities, a key math concept. This teacher measured degrees of temperature, but another teacher could as easily pick something else to measure in inches, feet, pounds, or seconds.

LEARNING TO SERIATE

An early example of seriation is often seen in the infant/toddler rooms, which usually have one or several sets of colorful stacking rings. When the rings are stacked properly on a central rod, they are arranged from largest at the bottom to smallest at the top. Watch the youngest children put the rings over the rod randomly with no consideration to order. As the child matures, the stacking becomes more thoughtful and intentional, although often not yet accurate. You can make it easier (more age appropriate) by putting out fewer rings, and making the rings differ greatly in size. Try providing other attractive toys to infants and toddlers that help develop seriation skills. These include stacking cups and stacking blocks. Keep in mind that these types of toys are hardly interesting to older children. Offer the same toy to a three-year-old, and she will be bored, handing it back completed in quick order.

Seriation: Ordering from Low to High

Just as young children begin with rough estimates of big and little and then progress to finer distinctions about size, the same progress can be seen in children's developing ability to seriate a set of objects. Seriation means to arrange objects into a logical order according to some characteristic, such as their size or weight. For example, a set of ten sticks, each one an inch longer than the previous one, can be seriated into a stair-step sequence. This kind of task is difficult for toddlers. If asked to arrange the sticks from shortest to longest, toddlers often simply divide them into a short pile and a long pile. With time, this expands to three piles, and then more experience leads them to create a fully seriated series.

Toddlers love to play with nesting bowls or boxes precisely because this activity requires the child to find the seriated sequence, from smallest to largest. This is a challenging and therefore involving task. In addition to nesting boxes and bowls, children can be given other types of seriation tasks besides size. A child can be challenged to order a set of bells from lowest to highest notes, or a set of color cards from lightest to darkest blue.

The numbers from one to ten are, of course, a seriated sequence (think of sticks that are one inch long, two inches long, up to ten inches long), so all these experiences with ordering objects help a child to develop a mature understanding of number.

PROMISING PRACTICE

Teaching Subtraction

What We Saw

Elisa wants to make a pegboard picture just like the one shown on the box. Teacher Hannah helps Elisa, because the pegs are difficult to push into place. Elisa counts the number of pegs in the picture, "One, two, three, four, five, six." Hannah asks, "How many are already in the pegboard?" Elisa answers, "Four." Hannah holds up six fingers, saying, "We need six, and we have four. One, two, three, four" as she puts down fingers, leaving two up. "So how many do we still need?" Elisa counts, "One, two. We need two more." She gives two pegs to Hannah to push into the frame.

What It Means

A good early childhood setting is rich in opportunities to solve problems, and solving problems is how children create knowledge. Elisa probably could not have solved this problem on her own, but with a little help from her teacher, she did. The teacher provides just enough additional, external structure (such as using fingers to represent the subtraction problem and posing the right question) so Elisa can discover the solution. From this experience, Elisa may need less help next time. That's teaching!

Development of Early Addition and Subtraction Skills

When most children are two-and-a-half to three years old, they begin to understand how to solve simple addition and subtraction problems if you demonstrate the problem in a way they can understand. In one study, children watched a researcher perform addition and subtraction problems using black discs (Huttenlocher, Jordan, and Levine 1994). For one addition problem, the researcher placed one black disk on a mat, covered the disk, and then placed another disk under the cover while the child watched. The child was then asked to put the same number of disks on her own mat so that when the researcher lifted the cover, the number of disks on both mats would match. A similar procedure was used for subtraction problems.

Most children younger than two and a half were not able to solve even the easiest problems such as 1 + 1 and 2 − 1, even when they were demonstrated with disks in this way. However, among children closer to three years of age, over half could solve both of these problems. Thus, children over two-and-a-half years are beginning to learn how to solve the simplest addition and subtraction problems. By the time they are almost four years old, two-thirds were successful with these simple problems, and some were beginning to correctly solve more difficult problems, such as 3 − 1, 3 − 2, 2 + 1, and 1 + 2.

Something interesting to note is that children tend to give the *same* wrong answers on these tests. This means their mistakes are not just random, but actually reflect a different way of thinking than adults use. In particular, young children's thinking is dominated by the visual appearance of things rather than logic. For example, over one-third of preschoolers' mistakes consisted of answering the problem with the same number of disks that the researcher had originally laid down, before adding or subtracting. Thus, rather than thinking about the logic of the task, the young children in the study focused on how many disks they had seen on the mat before they were covered. A key insight for teachers is that when children learn math, they are really learning logical thinking.

✔ *Practice Tip*

Experiencing Fractions

If a teacher tries, experiences with fractions can be worked into most early childhood activities. At lunch, ask the children if they would like ¼ glass more milk or ½ glass more. At the craft table, you might say, "Here Juan, I'll give you half the crayons and Reiko the other half."

Another way to understand fractions is to recognize the relationship of the part to the whole. Since pizza is a familiar food for many children, it can be the basis of a fun part-whole activity. Take a circular metal pizza tray (or other circular dish) and cut a variety of "pizzas" out of tagboard or cardboard. Start simple at first, with two half pizzas. Then work up to a ¾ pizza and a ¼ slice to complete the pizza. These are all easy, because they add only one part to create the whole. More difficult would be four equal slices to fit together for the whole pizza. (Several parts fit together to make the whole.)

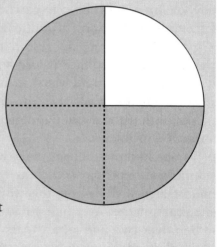

Preschoolers Begin to Develop Early Fraction Calculation Abilities

When we think of learning about fractions, grade school might come to mind. However, research shows that even preschoolers are learning to calculate simple fraction problems. In one study, three- to five-year-olds observed the researcher perform simple fraction problems using pieces of a circular sponge cut into four equal sections (Mix, Levine, and Huttenlocher 1999). For example, the researcher placed ¾ of the sponge in a tray as the child watched. A screen then covered the sponge and the researcher added another ¼ of the sponge while the child watched. The child was then shown four pictures—¼ of a circle, ½ of a circle, ¾ of a circle, and one whole circle—and was asked to choose which picture matched the amount behind the screen.

Three-year-olds did no better than chance on the fraction problems. They guessed at the answers. However, four- and five-year-olds answered more problems correctly than if they had just been guessing. This shows that preschoolers are just beginning to learn how to solve simple fraction problems.

Table 2.2: Development of Early Mathematical Skills

Age of child	Early mathematical skills
Newborn infant	• Can tell the difference between two and three objects (probably sees differences in amount of objects, rather than number of objects)
2¹/₂ to 3 years old	• When one to three objects present, recognizes number of objects without counting, through a process called subitizing • Begins to learn simple addition and subtraction, 1 + 1 and 2 − 1 • Learns to identify circles and squares
3¹/₂ to 4 years old	• Recognizes number of objects without counting for one to four objects • Begins to learn more complex addition and subtraction, 3 − 1 and 2 + 1 • Begins to learn the three counting principles: one-to-one correspondence, stable order, and cardinality • On average, the highest number children can count to is twelve before making mistakes (Murray and Mayer 1988) • Begins to learn to identify triangles and rectangles • Begins to understand differences between small (1, 2, 3, 4) and large (5, 6, 7, 8, 9) numbers
4 to 5 years old	• On average, the highest number children can count to is forty before making mistakes (Murray and Mayer 1988) • Begins to understand differences in number magnitude for small numbers (1, 2, 3, 4) • Begins to understand differences between small (1, 2, 3), medium (4, 5), and large numbers (6, 7, 8, 9) • Learns to calculate simple fraction problems such as two halves make a whole

Math Is Everywhere!

What We Saw

The teacher helps several children in a sorting activity with leaves they collected on a walk. She helps one child sort the leaves into two piles of yellow and brown. When another child decides to put her leaves away, the teacher encourages her to count them as she puts them in the bag. Together they count five. While they are counting, they talk about which leaves are big and which are small.

What It Means

A casual observer could easily miss how much math learning is taking place here. It begins with learning to classify objects into sets (yellow versus brown leaves). Then the principle of one-to-one correspondence (necessary for a full understanding of numbers) is emphasized by counting along with the child's own actions (putting each leaf in the bag). Finally, distinctions of quantity are made (how many big versus how many little). Next time, the teacher may also encourage the children to lay the leaves out from smallest to biggest: that's seriation, a step toward an understanding of numbers.

Promoting Math Development in Early Care and Education Programs

Preschoolers Make Fewer Counting Mistakes When They Can Touch the Objects They Are Counting

We have all seen children count or add on their fingers when they cannot yet do so inside their heads. In fact, this limitation to the concrete, touchable world extends to the counting of many objects. Children have difficulty counting objects they cannot feel, move, or easily point to with their fingers while counting. In one study, three- to four-year-olds were asked to count three-dimensional refrigerator magnets and two-dimensional stickers on a card (Gelman and Meck 1983). The children could easily touch both the magnets and the stickers while counting. Children were also asked to count the same magnets while they were under a Plexiglas cover that prevented the children from being able to touch them. The three-year-olds had more difficulty counting the magnets under the Plexiglas cover than counting the uncovered magnets or stickers, no matter how many objects were present to count. The four-year-olds also had more difficulty counting the magnets under the Plexiglas cover, but only when there were many objects to count (such as fifteen or nineteen objects).

We do not exaggerate in saying that young children first grasp numbers with their hands and only later grasp those same numbers with their minds. (The Italian educator, Maria Montessori, was the first to point this out.)

✔ *Practice Tip*

Using Words to Reinforce Math Concepts

Use words to describe and reinforce math concepts during your everyday interactions with children. The words you use to talk about the child's activity should match the child's level of understanding, beginning with simple terms and then gradually moving toward more complex labels for the concept the child is observing and exploring while playing.

Math concept:	Words to describe:
Quantity	more/less, some/a lot, few/many, 1, 2, 3 . . .
Distance	here/there, near/far, how far? (unit of measurement: inches, feet, and so forth)
Speed	slow/fast, how fast? (unit of measurement: seconds, minutes)
Sequence	my turn/your turn, first/next/last, first, second, third . . .
Classification	by any attribute: color, size, shape, height, weight, volume, and then by cross-classifications: blue and square, blue and round, red and square, red and round
Shape	two-dimensional shapes: round/straight, circle, square, triangle, ellipse, rhomboid, and so forth three-dimensional shapes: sphere, cube, cylinder, and so forth

Using Language Helps Children Classify Shapes Better

In one study, three- to six-year-olds were asked to pick out the triangles and rectangles from a variety of shapes (Hannibal 1999). When the children were asked to explain the reason why a shape was (or was not) a triangle or rectangle, they were more often correct (as compared to children who were not asked to explain their rationale). For example, the researchers might ask, "Why isn't that one a triangle?" or "How do you know that one is a rectangle?" These questions can help children think more carefully or even rethink their answers and respond correctly.

The Addition of Number-Related Dramatic Play Props Promotes Children's Number Talk and Number Play

In one research study, when a dramatic play area that emphasized numbers was added to classrooms in two different child care centers, number talk and number play increased among children (Cook 1996). The theme of the new dramatic play areas was a birthday party. Play materials included cards with numbers, pencils with blank cards, party plates and bowls, candles, and cake pans in the shapes of different numbers. Children's talk about numbers, quantities, comparisons of sizes or ages, time, and sharing all greatly increased in the dramatic play area after the addition of these materials.

✓ Practice Tip

Including Math in the Dramatic Play Area

Almost any dramatic play area can incorporate math concepts. A restaurant has a need for place settings that require counting dishes, silverware, and place mats. If pizza is the serving of the day, cardboard pizzas can be made and available to be divided into fractions. If the play center becomes a post office, letters can be addressed with numbers and zip codes. Mail can be counted and delivered, and packages or envelopes can be ordered by size and weight. Turn the area into a fitness center (we observed this in one program), and children can be measured and weighed. They can also count rotations of jumping or walking laps. The possibilities are endless!

Music Experiences Promote Math Skills

Researchers were surprised to discover, some years ago, that adult musicians score better on tests of one math skill—spatial thinking—than do nonmathematicians (Hassler, Birbaumer, and Fiel 1985). More surprising is that this can be seen even in novice musicians: preschoolers. Studies have found that preschoolers who have more music experiences at home do better on tests measuring early math skills (Georghegan and Mitchelmore 1996). Some studies have experimented, by increasing the music activities in some early childhood classrooms, to see if those children gained more in their understanding of math than did children in other classrooms. These studies have found that increasing the music activities leads to improvements in children's spatial intelligence, for example, children's ability to complete a puzzle, or recognize that two geometric designs are the same (Rauschler et al. 1997; Gromko and Poorman 1998).

Most studies finding that musical instruction causes improvements in spatial-mathematical reasoning have been of piano keyboard instruction. Since a keyboard is laid out in a linear sequence, like a number series, this makes sense. Another explanation for the link between music and math comes from recent research on brain functioning. Researchers have found that the same part of the brain is used for musical thinking and spatial-temporal thinking (Leng and Shaw 1991). This helps explain why instruction in one could lead to improvement in the other. (For more on the studies linking math and music, see chapter 3.)

Children's Math and Number Learning Is Promoted by Nurturing Environments and Hands-on Learning

Many studies have found that young children learn best through their own interactions with materials. They also learn best when their teachers interact with them, but do not take over completely. Children learn math and other concepts best when teachers prepare them with ideas in advance, and talk with them about what they are learning while (and after) they work with materials that present math problems (Mayer 2004).

In fact, children ages three to five who attended programs that provided these supportive and semi-structured learning environments scored higher on tests of their math and number skills than children the same age who attended programs that specifically focused on teaching basic skills (such as learning numbers and letters) by using worksheets or other teacher-directed activities (Stipek et al. 1998).

Fun with the *Stable Order Principle* of Counting

What We Saw

The teacher in the four-year-old class is playing a game she calls "Blast Off!" All the children are crouched down on the floor, and she leads them in counting backward from ten. She begins "ten, nine, eight." The children count with her, and when they get to zero, they all scream "Blast off!" and jump into the air. They yell to repeat the game, and she tells them to get into their launching position. They all crouch again, and this time she says, "ten, four, seven . . ." The children scream and stop her saying, "No, no, that's not how it goes." She asks for help, and they all count together to zero and once again blast off.

What It Means

By four years old, most children can comfortably count to ten, and they enjoy counting. This teacher added to the fun, by recognizing their need to be active, and used the countdown to keep their interest. By saying the numbers in the wrong order, she was helping the children learn the *stable order principle* that numbers must be counted in sequence both forward and backward.

Helping Parents Become Involved with Their Preschoolers Promotes Children's Mathematical Development

Children score better on tests of mathematical ability when their parents are involved with them at their early care and education programs *and* at home. In one study, a family mathematics class was offered to four- to five-year-old children attending a Head Start program (Starkey and Klein 2000). Participating children attended the math class with their mothers every other week for four months. The class was designed to help mothers participate in math activities with their children. After teachers demonstrated an activity, mothers and their children were given the materials to do the activity together. After each class, mothers had the opportunity to check out any of the materials from the math library so that activities could be repeated at home.

All of the children attending the Head Start program were tested on their math skills: once before the math classes began and again after the classes ended. Researchers found that children who had participated with their mothers in the math classes made significant improvements on the test. (The other children did not.) The mothers were the teachers in this study. When mothers became involved in playing math activities with their children, their children made much better progress in learning new math skills.

In another study, children whose fathers participated in a program at their children's Head Start program significantly improved their math test scores (Fagen and Iglesias 1999). During the program, fathers were encouraged to volunteer in their children's preschool classrooms. Fathers also could participate in weekly father-child reading in the classrooms and father-child outings, such as cookouts in the park or trips to the pool. Finally, fathers were encouraged to attend a support group every month designed for them to talk about parenting. Children made significant improvements on math tests when fathers participated in the various program components for an extensive period of time (at least twenty-one hours or more), even though most of the activities were not specifically about math.

Just as with early literacy skills, children from low-income households tend to be less advanced in math abilities than their middle class peers (Ginsburg, Klein, and Starkey 1998). One reason is that their home environments tend to provide less stimulation of math reasoning. Researchers find that although low-income parents tend to encourage traditional math skills (for example, number and shape recognition), they provide fewer opportunities for their children to practice more complex math reasoning (Saxe, Guberman, and Gearhart 1987). When children's home environments lack this math stimulation, it is all the more important for their preschool classrooms to provide it.

MISTAKEN PRACTICE

Using Worksheets to Teach Math

Why This Happens

Most adults remember having to do worksheets in school. They are familiar, easy to find, inexpensive, and take little time and effort to provide for children. They also result in a document to send home to families that shows evidence of "teaching math" in your program.

What Would Work Better

Provide a variety of objects for hands-on exploration and discovery of the principles of math. Children need lots of experience manipulating collections of objects—to sort, classify, arrange, count, compare, gather, and distribute. We want children to understand the math concepts, not just memorize the right answers. Concrete experiences are required for this. Being able to touch and manipulate real items allows for trial and experimentation of materials in order to discover the logic that is the foundation of mathematical understanding.

Children's Experiences in Early Care and Education Programs Affect Their Future Math Abilities

Early care and education programs not only affect children's early development of number skills, but also appear to contribute to children's later mathematical abilities. In fact, research shows that children's experiences during early childhood influence their math abilities in grade school, high school, and beyond.

Research suggests that children experiencing greater amounts of construction play (working with shapes and quantities) may be laying a foundation for better math understanding in middle school and high school (Stannard, Wolfgang, Jones, and Phelps 2001). In this research study, three- to four-year-olds' block play, Lego play, and carpentry was observed at their early care and education program. Each type of play was rated according to its complexity and its use of materials in creative ways. These construction play scores were later compared to children's math performance in grades three through high school. After taking into consideration the effects of IQ and gender on children's math achievement, researchers found that scores on all three construction tasks predicted children's seventh grade math scores and high school math grades. Children who received higher scores on the block play, Lego play, and carpentry task in preschool were more likely to have higher math test scores in middle school and higher math grades in high school. These children were also more likely to take courses in higher mathematics in high school.

This research wasn't an experiment, so it doesn't prove that the early construction play caused the later math abilities. For example, an alternative explanation for these findings could be that both the pre-school construction play and the later math abilities were caused by an underlying, inborn ease with math. On the other hand, any inborn potential requires the right kinds of experiences to be realized, and construction play offers young children a wealth of raw experience with shapes, quantities, and relationships—the foundation of mathematical thinking.

Studies have also found that children attending high-quality early care and education programs had higher math achievement than other children had when they were older. In one study, children had higher math grades in sixth grade if they had spent a longer period of time attending full-time high quality early care and education programs during early childhood (Field 1991). The high-quality child care programs had fewer children per teacher, high levels of teacher training and experience, and low levels of teacher turnover.

In another study, children from low-income families who attended a full-time, high-quality early care and education program from infancy through age five scored better on math achievement tests at ages eight, twelve, fifteen, and twenty-one than did children not attending the program (Campbell et al. 2001). Researchers found that this difference was due in large part to children's increased cognitive abilities after participating in the high-quality child care program. The early childhood program had low caregiver-to-child ratios, low caregiver turnover, and well-trained staff. The program also emphasized a developmentally appropriate curriculum that included playing with infants to promote their cognitive, social, language, and perceptual-motor development. The preschool curriculum focused on helping children learn language and literacy skills.

Playing with blocks has long been a central activity of play-oriented early childhood programs, and researchers have studied the complexity of children's block play, and whether complexity predicts later math skills. It does! More complex block play predicted better math performance in both middle school and high school. Even when they compared children of equal IQ in early childhood, those with more complex block play had better math performance in high school (Wolfgang, Stannard, and Jones 2001). While constructing things with blocks, children can classify, order, count, measure, and work with the spatial reasoning concepts of length, width, height, shape, and symmetry (Hirsch 1996).

Early care and education programs may have especially large impacts on math learning because children receive so little elsewhere. In a study of children's everyday involvement in learning activities or play in their homes, researchers discovered that parents frequently engaged children in literacy activities, but seldom in activities involving mathematics (Tudge and Doucet 2004). This makes the early childhood classroom all the more important.

Practice Tip

Using Signs with Numbers

If your classroom is divided into learning stations, consider hanging a sign at each area with a number and a representation of that number in dots that indicates how many children may play in that learning station at a time. Seeing the number represented in both written and dot form helps children see the *one-to-one correspondence* between the number of dots and the number of children allowed in the learning station.

Practice Tip

Voting as Math

Children will really pay attention to votes if they are about something they care about, such as their favorite color or which dessert to have. When taking a vote in class, teacher-caregivers should take the time to help children understand the meaning of "more" votes versus "less" votes, and how each corresponds to the classroom decision.

Conclusion

From an early age, children are interested in shapes, quantities, and numbers. Even newborns have some informal math ability (recognizing greater and lesser amounts of things). In early childhood, the foundation of a child's later math abilities is laid through everyday interactions with materials through which children learn about quantity, speed, distance, classification, patterns, shapes, space, and sequence. These are the building blocks from which children develop their own understandings of mathematical relationships, first on the concrete level and then increasingly through the invention of abstract principles (such as one-to-one correspondence, and the stable order principle). Long before teachers begin to instruct them in our formal, codified version of math, children are developing their own intuitive understandings of the principles of math.

If you just observe everyday play, you will see children using math intuitively. The trend in their understanding is from perceptual to logical, from seeing the appearance of things to understanding the underlying regularities of math.

Teachers can build on the interests of children and promote early mathematical skills by encouraging mathematical talk and activities and incorporating mathematical materials into daily play. Children advance much further in their early math learning if they are provided with a prepared early childhood environment that creates opportunities for math learning and then given some guidance by a teacher. Promoting math learning in early care and education programs will not only help children develop math skills as preschoolers, but will also provide children with a strong foundation for later mathematics success during grade school, high school, and early adulthood.

Further Reading

On Research

Baroody, A. J. 2000. Does mathematics instruction for three- to five-year-olds really make sense? *Young Children* 55 (4): 61–67.

Ginsburg, H. P., A. Klein, and P. Starkey. 1998. The development of children's mathematical thinking: Connecting research with practice. In *Handbook of Child Psychology*, Vol. 4, volume editors I. E. Sigel and K. A. Renninger, series editor W. Damon, 401–476. New York: Wiley.

Hilton, S. C., S. D. Grimshaw, and G. T. Anderson. 2001. Statistics in preschool. *American Statistician* 55 (4): 332–336.

On Practice

Bankauskas, D. 2000. Teaching chess to young children. *Young Children* 55(4): 33.

Copley, J. V. 2000. *The young child and mathematics*. Washington, D.C.: National Association for the Education of Young Children and National Council of Teachers of Mathematics.

Geist, E. 2001. Children are born mathematicians: Promoting the construction of early mathematical concepts in children under five. *Young Children* 56 (4): 12–19.

Greenberg, P. 1993. Ideas that work with young children: How and why to teach all aspects of preschool and kindergarten math naturally, democratically, and effectively (for teachers who don't believe in academic programs, who do believe in educational excellence, and who find math boring to the max)—Part 1. *Young Children* 48:75–84.

Hirsch, E. 1996. *The block book.* Washington D.C.: National Association for the Education of Young Children.

Hohman, M., and D. Weikart. 2002. *Educating young children: Active learning practices for preschool and child care programs.* Ypsilanti MI: High-Scope Press.

Nelson, G. 2007. *Math at their own pace: Child-directed math activities for developing early number sense.* Saint Paul, MN: Redleaf Press.

Thatcher, D. H. 2001. Reading in the math class: Selecting and using picture books for math investigations. *Young Children* 56 (4): 20–27.

Wallace, A. H., D. Abbott, and R. M. Blary. 2007. The classroom that math built: Encouraging young mathematicians to pose problems. *Young Children* 62 (5): 42–48.

Children's Books

Allen, P. 1982. *Who sank the boat?* New York: Coward-McCann.

Anno, M. 1977. *Anno's counting book.* New York: HarperCollins.

Archambault, J. 2004. *Boom chicka rock.* New York: Philomel Books.

Bang, M. 1983. *Ten, nine, eight.* New York: Greenwillow Books.

Boynton, S. 1996. *Hippos go beserk!* New York: Simon & Schuster.

Burns, M. 1994. *The greedy triangle.* New York: Scholastic.

Cohen, C. L. 1996. *Where's the fly?* New York: Greenwillow Books.

Cronin, D. 2006. *Clic, clac, plif, plaf: Una adventura de contar* (Click, clack, splish, splash: A counting adventure). New York: Lectorum.

Ehlert, L. 1990. *Fish eyes: A book you can count on.* San Diego: Harcourt Brace Jovanovich.

Franco, B. 1997. *Sorting all sorts of socks.* Alpharetta, GA: Creative Publications.

Grossman, V. 1991. *Ten little rabbits*. San Francisco: Chronicle Books.

MacDonald, S. 1994. *Sea shapes*. San Diego: Harcourt Brace.

McBratney, S. 1994. *Guess how much I love you*. Cambridge, MA: Candlewick Press.

McGrath, B. B. 1998. *The Cheerios counting book*. New York: Scholastic.

Plummer, D., and J. Archambault. 1997. *Counting kittens*. Lancaster, PA: Childcraft.

~~~~~~

When Teachers Reflect: *Are You Afraid of Math?*

Some early childhood teachers do not feel confident in their ability to teach mathematics, and either shy away from opportunities or resort to numbered flash cards or workbook pages. Have no fear. You are probably teaching math already, without realizing it.

Do you sing songs with the children, such as "The ants go marching one by one"? That song teaches counting, so you are teaching math. When several children want to play with the same toy, do you suggest that Amy goes first and Victor is second? It is math in evidence again. You are teaching sequence. Think about what you do during your center activities, and try to see how math is being demonstrated. Small manipulatives, block play, dramatic play, and art projects can all have a mathematical twist when looked at with math in mind. If a child is drawing a house, how many windows does it have? If children are building a bridge with blocks, which ones are the biggest, the same color, the same shape?

The classroom abounds in opportunities to teach math concepts. You just need to recognize them, and intentionally put them to use.

~~~~~~

When Teachers Reflect: *Making Math a Part of Your Everyday Thinking*

We often think of math as something we need to plan separately, when it is really something that can be easily incorporated into daily routines and activities. Think about your day and answer the following questions:

- How can you incorporate counting into mealtime?

- How can estimation be a daily part of circle time?

- How can learning centers be enhanced with math concepts?

- What kinds of open-ended questions can you ask to help children think more about math concepts?

- How can you educate parents on ways to enhance math awareness at home?

When Teachers Reflect: Cooking as a Way to Learn Math

Young children love to eat what they have made! Cooking is a great way to incorporate mathematical concepts and have lots of fun doing so. Concepts such as quantity, number, counting, and one-to-one correspondence come alive when a large recipe chart is used for children to reference as they are involved in a cooking project. Measuring cups and spoons are a great way to learn about quantities and how to use tools to measure. Fruits and vegetables are a colorful way to sort and classify objects by a variety of properties. A taste testing of apple varieties can become a way to chart or graph various properties.

- How can you include cooking experiences into your lesson plan?

- In what ways can you include printed materials to increase math competence?

- What kinds of questions can you ask children while cooking to increase their knowledge of mathematical concepts?

For a wide variety of recipes and tips, consult *The cooking book: Fostering young children's learning and delight* by Laura J. Colker.

Letter to Parents

Did You Know?

From an early age, children are interested in numbers, shapes and quantities, and have some intuitive understandings of mathematics.

Did You Know?

Children who are better at early mathematical abilities tend to learn math more easily in their school years?

Did You Know?

Children score better on tests of mathematical ability when their parents are involved with them at their early education programs and at home.

Did You Know?

We incorporate mathematical concepts into many of our daily activities. The songs we sing and games we play often involve counting, categorizing into sets, ordering according to size, separating a whole into parts, adding into a sum, identifying geometrical shapes, and similar mathematical concepts. You can do the same at home with your child.

Put Math into Action:

- Count stairs as you walk.
- Let children match socks.
- Set the table with your child, having her count the place settings or napkins.
- Look for patterns in the world around you: leaves that match, squares on the sidewalk, colors of cars.

You will be helping in the development of skills that will provide your child with a foundation for later mathematics success during grade school, high school, and beyond.

From *Intellectual Development: Connecting Science and Practice in Early Childhood Settings* (Redleaf Press, 2009).

© 2009 by Dave Riley, Mary Carns, Ann Ramminger, Joan Klinkner, and Colette Sisco.

Why We Sing Throughout the Day

The Development of Musical Ability

Cynthia, a caregiver in a toddler room, has just an-
nounced that it's time to go outside. The toddlers rush to
put on their coats and hats for the cold winter air. There
are many pleas for help, and Dave, another caregiver,
is busily circulating from child to child to help zip, tie,
and buckle. Some children are faster than others and are
becoming restless to get outside. "Let's sing a song while
we wait for everyone to get ready!" Cynthia exclaims.
"Spider!" Becky shouts. Cynthia begins singing "The
Itsy Bitsy Spider," and the children join in on the move-
ments. After another song, everyone is bundled up, and
they head outside.

Music, like language, is a universal human characteristic. In fact, every known culture develops its own lullabies, finger plays, and songs for babies and young children. It is a form of communication that begins long before babies understand language. Caregivers in all cultures sing to infants as part of their everyday routines (Trehub and Trainor 1998). Without being taught, humans love the sound of music—right from birth. And music is also one of those fields of human achievement in which genius can be spotted early.

Howard Gardner, a prominent scientist who studies intelligence, believes that there are multiple "intelligences," not just a single IQ, and that musical/rhythmic thinking is one of the nine primary forms of intelligence (Gardner 1999). He also suggests that music may act to organize our thinking processes, and this may be especially true for children. As we will see in this chapter, recent research has found evidence that musical experience does lead to gains in other areas of children's intelligence, including pre-reading and mathematical learning.

Music is a daily part of good early care and education programs. It is often used during transition times, as in the above example, during routines (such as diaper changing, hand washing, or naptime) and as a group activity. Music can be used to calm children or to focus their attention. Musical activities are versatile because they can be implemented in large or small groups or with individual children. Exposing children to music is good for developing musical appreciation and ability, and it also contributes to other aspects of children's development, including their physical, language, reading, and math abilities.

PROMISING PRACTICE
The Universal Experience of Lullabies

What We Saw

While the teacher fed the infant, she gently massaged his head and sang softly. She sang the word "mama" going up and down the musical scale. The boy visibly relaxed in her arms, gazing at her face while she hummed. As he relaxed more, the teacher murmured, "Almost done, going to sleep, getting sleepy, did your mommy wake you up so early?" The child fell asleep, and the teacher held him for awhile longer, softly humming. Still humming, she carried him to his crib.

What It Means

There is something so reassuring, almost nourishing, about music used in this way. We know that nursery lullabies are a human universal: parents in every human culture sing them to their babies. Using song in this way is like pulling a blanket over a cold child, or feeding a hungry child, or hugging a frightened child. If the caregivers of infants don't sing to them, we might wonder if all the child's needs are really being met. This child was being fed, but also emotionally nourished.

✔ *Practice Tip*

Using Voices Infants Know

Partner with Parents

Ask parents (grandparents or other family members) to tape themselves singing to their infants. The tape can be used to soothe the child who is upset or who is trying to fall asleep at naptime.

Become a Famous Recording Artist (to the Children in Your Class)

Tape yourself singing, and then play it to a child when you cannot attend to him or her immediately. Who knows, they may ask to listen to your tape during free playtime!

Tape Record the Infants Themselves

Tape them when they are happy and engaged, then play it back to them. Watch their reactions!

Musical Development in Early Childhood

Babies Like to Listen to Us Sing

Right from the start, babies are attuned to the sounds around them, paying attention to the patterns of music and expressing preferences for some sounds over others. Immediately after birth, babies already prefer the sound of their own mother's voice over that of a stranger's (probably because they have heard it so often in the previous months!) (DeCasper and Fifer 1980).

When adults of every culture sing to babies, they sound very different than when singing to themselves, much as adults of every culture use a special way of talking (parentese) with babies (O'Neill, Trainor, and Trehub 2001; Trainor 1996). To study this, researchers asked parents to sing a nursery song, such as "Row, Row, Row Your Boat," once to their babies and once while pretending to be in the shower or car singing to themselves. College students were then asked to identify which taped songs were sung to infants. Approximately 90 percent of the songs sung to infants were correctly identified. Students said these songs had a "softer voice," a "smiling tone," and a "slower pace."

Do infants prefer to listen to the songs that parents and caregivers sing just for them? Research has found that six-month-old babies do listen longer to songs that mothers sing to them than to songs the mothers sing when alone, when both are played on tapes (Trainor 1996). The same was also true for fathers' songs, but only when the pitch of fathers' voices was digitally raised.

Most surprising was research on the "singing" of deaf mothers to their babies. Just like songs to babies, their signed messages to their babies tended to be more rhythmic, repetitive, and emotionally expressive than their signed messages to adults (Masataka 1999). We might say that instead of singing, they danced (with their hands) for their babies.

One of the most interesting findings about babies' musical preferences is that they prefer love songs. When we say "love songs," we don't just mean songs about love, but songs that are sung in a loving tone and manner. The more loving the singer's tone of voice (according to adults who rated tapes of the singing), the longer babies chose to listen to the taped song in an experiment (Trainor 2002).

THE COMFORT OF A FAMILIAR SONG

In studies of mothers singing to their children at home, researchers find that most mothers have a small number of songs that they sing repeatedly. More surprising, the mothers tend to sing the songs exactly the same every time (the same pitch, tempo, and words) (Bergeson and Trehub 2002). This makes sense, if you think about it. A consistent song becomes a familiar source of security for the child, in the same way that regular routines or a "security blanket" can make a child feel secure. A consistent routine is easy and probably provides the parent with comfort too.

Of course, if your coworker were to sing the same song all day long, in exactly the same way, it might drive you crazy! Fortunately, most caregivers learn a wide selection of songs. Still, you may find that you use a particular song for the same situation each day. For example, you may have a song you sing while diapering or while putting children to sleep. This makes sense: it calms children by making their day more predictable and understandable.

Fussy Baby? We Prescribe Lullabies

Singing may be one of the best ways to soothe a crying baby or even a tired toddler. When we sing lullabies, our soft and soothing voices will help a child relax. Singing may also help reduce the anxiety that children feel when another child is upset. In fact, lullabies may even help *us* remain calm while trying to comfort a crying child!

Do you feel uncomfortable singing alone? Are you unsure of what songs to sing? Try singing along with one of the lullaby tapes you use for naptime. Although at first you may not know all the words, just humming softly will help to soothe babies. Soon you will have picked up the words and may not even need the tape for accompaniment.

Singing Is Preverbal Communication

Both mothers and fathers put more emotional feeling into their voices when they sing to babies (Trehub et al. 1997). Even preschoolers sing with more emotionality when they are asked to sing to a baby brother or sister (Trehub, Unyk, and Henderson 1994).

The feeling we put into our songs has a real effect on babies. You may have noticed how one baby will start crying when she hears another baby cry, a process we call "emotional contagion" (Hatfield, Cacioppro, and Rapson 1994). The same thing happens in song, with the baby adopting the same calm, positive feeling that the caregiver communicates through voice. Research has shown that maternal singing calms infants, and because infants are also very attentive to the singing of other caregivers, we think that singing by children's caregivers is also likely to calm infants (Trehub 2002).

While many of our songs to babies are calming lullabies, other songs are invitations to play (play songs). Researchers have found that adults can easily distinguish between these two types of songs, and these two types of songs have very different effects on babies. Lullabies calm babies, but when babies hear play songs, they look up and around the room, as if they expect something interesting to happen. Observers could consistently tell which type of song was being played for a baby, even though they couldn't hear the songs, just by watching the baby's response (Trainor 2002).

PITCH

Often we provide for children musical instruments that have a very high pitch. This high pitch, combined with the general background noise of a classroom, leads some teachers to avoid musical activities. Caregivers also sometimes find themselves struggling to find the pitch that is comfortable for them when attempting to sing along with high-pitched children's CDs.

Music doesn't have to be loud or high pitched. Many wooden drums have a mellow sound. Wooden xylophones allow children to explore the scale without adding metallic tones to the classroom.

Babies Pay Attention to Patterns in Music

To explore babies' understanding of patterns in music, researchers examined whether babies prefer to listen to music that contains pauses at the end of musical phrases or to music that contains pauses that interrupt musical phrases (Krumhansl and Jusczyk 1990). A musical phrase is like a sentence for music. Just as in conversations, pauses usually occur at the end of the phrase (or sentence). For example, the sentence "She took the cat to the vet" would sound odd to us if we heard it this way: "She took the [pause] cat to the vet." Researchers found that both four-and-a-half- and six-month-old infants listened longer to music with pauses at the end of musical phrases than to music with pauses in the middle. Babies already have an opinion about the music they prefer to listen to, and just like us, they prefer music that pauses at the natural breaks at the end of musical phrases.

Besides recognizing natural phrases in music, babies also seem to pay attention to the contour of music. Music's contour is the up-and-down pattern that the notes in a song follow. For example, in "Twinkle, Twinkle, Little Star," the first six notes (twin-kle, twin-kle, lit-tle) go up the scale, or get progressively higher, and the next eight notes (star, how I won-der what you are) go down the scale, or get progressively lower. Researchers found that even babies as young as eight to ten months could tell the difference between songs in which the contour was modified from the original song (when notes in the song went up when they were supposed to go down) (Trehub, Bull, and Thorpe 1984).

Preschoolers are even more advanced at hearing musical patterns than infants are. Just like babies, preschoolers recognize changes in song contour. Unlike infants, preschoolers are able to notice when a single note is changed within the contour (Trehub, Bull, and Thorpe 1985).

RHYTHM

Rhythm is a sound pattern that repeats. One classic rhythm song is

Miss Mary Mack
All dressed in black,
With silver buttons,
All down her back.

The rhythm of this song captures children's interest. Clap your hands to the beat, and see if the children can follow. This can help them with their syllable segmentation skills. (See chapter 1 on early literacy skills.)

See the suggestions for sources of great songs at the end of this chapter.

Toddlers Begin to Sing, and Their Songs Increase in Complexity

Children usually begin to sing between the ages of one and two years (Dowling 2001). One group of researchers followed the development of singing in nine children from when they were one-year-olds until they were five-year-olds (Davidson 1985). They found that most children learned to sing in a predictable way. First, children learned parts of songs that included musical "leaps" across several notes. That is, children first learn to sing larger intervals. An interval is the distance (or musical difference) between two notes. For example, in the song "Row, row, row your boat," children might at first find it easier to sing the "merrily, merrily, merrily, merrily" part of the song because the distance between these notes is greater than in other parts of the song. Later, children learn to sing the parts with musical "steps," or smaller changes in notes between words. The "row your boat," "gently down the stream," and "life is but a dream" parts of the song are good examples of singing in steps. Each note is followed by another note that is only a little bit higher or lower (one musical step above or below the first note). You may have noticed this is similar to how young children learn numbers. (See chapter 2.) With numbers, children begin by noticing large differences (big and little), then begin to notice and use smaller differences. Eventually, they can seriate a set of objects (sticks or cups) from smallest to largest, much as they begin to notice smaller musical steps, and learn to arrange a set of bells from lowest pitch to highest.

The same researchers also discovered that some children developed an understanding of musical scales by being taught traditional songs (such as "Mary had a little lamb"), whereas other children seemed to come upon this knowledge simply by singing and practicing their own made-up songs (such as unrehearsed songs that children might sing to themselves while playing) (Davidson 1985). Both types of singing can be encouraged and supported in early care and education programs.

✔ Practice Tip

Having Fun with Mistakes!

Once children know and love a familiar song, it is great fun to make mistakes and let them teach you the right words. For example:

> "The itsy-bitsy spider went down the water spout . . ."
>   (Children: "No, UP the spout.")
> "Down came the snow"
>   (Children, laughing: "Rain!")
> "and washed the spider out.
> Out came the moon"
>   (Children, amazed at your apparent forgetfulness:
>   "Sun!")
> "And dried up all the rain,
> And the itsy-bitsy spider flew up the spout again."
>   (Children: "Not flew, it crawled!")

This is enormous fun. Being able to correct you also gives children a sense of mastery over the song, and it teaches them to listen carefully and thoughtfully. You are even teaching them linked concepts, like up-down, rain-snow, sun-moon, and fly-crawl.

Promoting Children's Musical Development and Musical Appreciation

Home Environments Influence Children's Musical Development

Why are some children already more advanced than others in their musical skills? When researchers asked teachers to rate the musical ability of four- to six-year-olds, and then followed these children home, they found that those with the greatest musical abilities had much more musically stimulating environments at home (Doxey and Wright 1990). In one study, researchers examined children's music environments at home by asking parents to rate their attitudes toward and encouragement of music (for example, "I feel that children should be given the opportunity to play a musical instrument if they want") and to rate their music behaviors (for example, "I usually listen to music when I am involved in other activities"). They also asked parents about the availability of music in their home (for example the number of musical instruments in their home and the number of CDs they purchased during the previous year). Children received higher ratings of music ability from their teachers if their parents had encouraged them to be involved in music activities, if

☑ *Practice Tip*

Encouraging Music at Home

Every month you can send home the lyrics to a few songs or fingerplays that you have been singing with the children. As children become familiar with the songs, they may begin to sing them and even teach them to family members at home. Encourage the parents to learn the words and sing along with their children.

Allow children to take home special "instrument bags" for a week. These bags could include instruments such as tambourines, maracas, xylophones, triangles, and wooden sticks that the children have already used in the classroom. Encourage family members to play along with children at home.

At a parent meeting, everyone can make musical instruments for their children. Decorate round oatmeal boxes for drums. Put gravel or other small items into plastic bottles, cap the top, and you have maracas. Experiment with different sized bottles, and different items inside, to make different sounds. Can you attach something to the edge of a plastic plate to make a tambourine?

Offer children and families the opportunity to borrow CDs or tapes from the classroom music library. Make sure there are various types of music available, such as classical, folk, children's groups, and ethnic music.

their parents were often involved in music activities themselves, and if children had music available at home. Therefore, teachers should be able to foster the development of children's music abilities by encouraging parents to create musical environments at home and by creating such an environment in their early care and education programs.

☑ *Practice Tip*

Bringing Music from the Children's Homes into Your Classroom

If you send music home, you may find that parents then offer to loan the classroom their own music. Because people love music, and love sharing it, music is one of the easiest ways to connect with the home cultures of the families you serve and to bring their home cultures into your classroom. Music can be a common ground on which we can meet and get to know one another. This year you may be lucky enough to listen to pan flutes from the Andes or to Jewish kletzmer music and get to know the families as well as their music.

Singing at Earlier Ages Is Related to Later Musical Ability

As with other parts of child development (such as language development or skill with math), early development tends to predict later development. So it should be no surprise that children who sing at earlier ages are found to be more successful at music in grade school and high school than children who begin to sing later.

In one research study (Howe, Davidson, Moore, and Sloboda 1995), children ages eight to eighteen who were admitted into a special music school because of their musical ability and potential were compared with children who had learned to play musical instruments but had been less successful. Parents were asked to remember when their children first danced to music, showed a preference for music, were attentive to music, requested to participate in music activities, and began to sing. The only significant difference between children who were more or less successful with music was the age at which children first began to sing. Forty percent of children with greater musical abilities sang before they were two years old, whereas only 25 percent of children who were less musically successful sang before they were two.

This finding might be explained by children with more innate (inborn) musical talent tending to sing at earlier ages. But it is also possible that early singing is a reflection of the child growing up in a music-rich environment. When researchers examined this question, they found that children who sang at earlier ages were also more likely than other children to have had frequent exposure to at least four other types of musical experiences with their parents at early ages. These parent-initiated musical activities included singing children to sleep, singing to them at other times, moving with them to music, engaging in musical play, and listening to music with their children. Therefore, regularly engaging in a variety of these types of musical activities when children are very young may turn out to pave the way for later musical brilliance. No doubt, some children are born with innate musical potential (Mozart began composing minuets by age six!), but it also appears that the early environment plays a role in molding that potential.

Musical Activities Can Help Children Learn Musical Concepts

Children tend to learn some musical concepts more easily than others. Research shows that preschoolers generally find it easy to understand differences in dynamics (loud versus soft) and tempo (fast versus slow) (Lawton and Johnson 1992). This suggests that these concepts should be the earliest focus of musical activities with young children. On the other hand, understanding pitch (high versus low) and rhythm (sound patterns that repeat over and over again) are more difficult concepts for preschoolers.

Can you really teach musical concepts, or is it better to just expose children to lots of music? Researchers contrasted two different music programs for four-year-olds at the Laboratory Preschool of the University of Wisconsin-Madison to test whether one or the other of these music programs was better at helping children understand musical concepts (Lawton and Johnson 1992). One program emphasized a different musical concept each week. The teacher began the activity by talking about the concept, using her voice and other instruments to demonstrate it. The teacher also used various pictures to demonstrate the concept (for example, a sleeping face for soft sounds and a surprised face for loud sounds). The teacher talked about how to make these different sounds and finally gave children the opportunity to practice the musical concept, using different instruments. This teacher was using "advance organizer" instruction methods: preparing children with the concepts to be learned prior to their hands-on experiences.

In the second program, the children spent just as much time on music activities, but the teacher did not specifically emphasize the musical concepts at the beginning of each session. Instead, the teacher conducted general musical activities with the children (for example, marching or playing instruments) and would mention musical concepts only when it fit with the activities taking place. (When children were pretending to be bunnies, the teacher mentioned that the music was soft.) Both of these programs took place every week for sixteen weeks, thirty minutes each week.

Following the sixteen weeks of music activities, children in the advance-organizer program had significantly improved their scores on tests of their understanding of pitch and rhythm, the more difficult concepts. Children in the music-exposure-only group did not improve on these tests. This research suggests that when teachers in early care and education settings specifically talk to children about musical concepts and provide musical activities for children to experience these concepts, preschoolers find it easier to understand these complex concepts.

✔ Practice Tip

Helping Children Listen Carefully

One fun way to encourage children to listen carefully to music is to record their own singing on tape. Children love the chance to sing into a microphone and are later excited to hear the sound of their own voices. For an added thrill, let the children dress up (in your dress-up play corner) before being recorded!

You can make one or two tape recorders available in a "listening center" so children can record and listen to themselves independently during free playtime. Use headphones if this creates too much noise in the room. Children could even have their own tapes, labeled with their names, so they can take their tapes home and show off their musical talents to their parents. Tell parents that a copy of this tape makes a great gift for grandparents.

Encouraging Children to Listen Carefully Promotes Preschoolers' Music Skills

Music can be presented to children in many different ways. How does the presentation of music affect children's learning of different skills? To find out, researchers examined four different ways of presenting music during music class (Persellin 1994). Four- to five-year-old children were randomly assigned into four groups that differed on the type of music instruction that children would receive twice per week for fifteen minutes. In the visual group, children were presented with visual drawings of the melodies and rhythms that they were singing and hearing as well as with pictures of things that they were singing and hearing about in the music. In the kinesthetic group, children were encouraged to move to the music while they were singing and hearing the music. In the auditory group, children sang and were encouraged to listen to the music. Finally, in the multimodal group, children were shown drawings and pictures, encouraged to move, and encouraged to listen to the music.

Before instruction began, children's abilities to remember and recognize melodies and rhythms were tested. For both the melody and rhythm tests, children heard three notes. Then three more notes were played and children were asked if they were the same or different. After ten weeks, these two tests were repeated. Children's abilities to match pitch were also tested by asking children to copy the singing of the two notes in "hello" that the researcher sang to the children. After the music instruction, the scores on the melody and rhythm tests increased significantly for children in the auditory and multimodal groups. Children in the visual group improved their scores only on the rhythm test, and children in the kinesthetic group did not improve on either test. Children in the auditory and multimodal groups were also better at matching pitches than children in the visual and kinesthetic groups. For the development of music skills, this study found that encouraging children to listen carefully and sing to the music really works. Encouraging children's creative movement and using visual materials with music are great ways to present music (they can make it more interesting) as long as really listening to the music is also encouraged.

✔ *Practice Tip*

Listening to Music

Dynamics of Music: Loud and Soft

An easy way to expose children to the dynamics of music is to sing songs (or parts of songs) in a range from very soft to very loud. Children love being allowed to be really loud, and making the transition to a softer voice helps them learn self-control.

"The Itsy-Bitsy Spider" is a favorite song for many. Children can be the Great Big Spider (with a deep loud voice) or the Teeny Tiny Spider (with a soft, whispered voice).

Tempo of Music

A good example of an activity that varies in tempo is the song "We're going on a bear hunt." To be fair to all members of the animal kingdom, you could also try going on a hunt for other animals that you could pretend to save or adopt for a make-believe school pet.

Any song can be varied in tempo. Singing a song faster, and then slower, is another terrific way to help young children learn to self-regulate their behaviors. Clap your hands or beat a drum to help emphasize the change in tempo.

Exposure to Varied Music Affects Preschoolers' Musical Preferences

To find out how exposure to varied music might affect preschoolers' musical preferences, researchers asked two groups of four-year-olds to rate how well they liked selected classical music pieces (by Vivaldi, Mozart, Beethoven, and Schubert) and popular pieces (a Sesame Street song and a TV theme song). At this age, children liked both types of music, but did not show a strong preference for one style of music over the other.

After this initial rating, the first group of children attended a weekly forty-five-minute music class for ten months. In the class, children were encouraged to engage in classical music experiences such as listening to and singing classical music, playing musical games, and learning the names of instruments in the orchestra. High school students also came to the class to show their instruments, and the children had the opportunity to play them. The second group of children did not participate in the structured musical training class, although they typically had some music activities as part of their early childhood program.

After ten months had passed, when the children were five years old, they were again asked how well they liked the classical and popular music pieces. Children in both groups again rated the popular music very highly. However, children's ratings of the classical pieces were significantly different. Preschoolers who had more experience with classical music at their early care and education programs continued to like classical music as much as they liked popular music, whereas preschoolers who did not have this experience showed less interest in classical music (Peery and Peery 1986). We suspect that the researchers would have found similar results for children's exposure to jazz, blues, or other musical styles.

✅ *Practice Tip*

Making Music Familiar

Children like familiar music, and music becomes familiar only when children hear it often enough. The meaning of the research finding on learning to like classical music (in the paragraph on this page) is not that we should promote classical music, but rather that we should expand children's exposure to music beyond children's songs and top-forty radio tunes. Teachers can promote children's (and their own) interest in classical music, jazz, folk, blues, reggae, ethnic music, and any other style by playing them in the classroom. Teachers can also offer a wide variety of music at listening centers that children can use independently. Exposure to different styles of music will help children appreciate and love music of all kinds.

Experiences with Music Promote Children's Development in Many Other Areas

Music Encourages Children's Physical Development

Children who often experience music at their early care and education programs have more opportunities to engage in movement and other physical activities than children who receive less exposure to music. In one observational research study, five- to twelve-month-old babies who were exposed to more singing and music activities at their child care center made almost twice as many rhythmic movements than babies who had fewer music experiences (Forrai 1997). Babies made the most movements when caregivers sang while children held an object that they could shake or sway. During these times, children often shook their hands or arms or rocked their bodies back and forth. One- to three-year-old toddlers who were exposed to more music also made more rhythmic movements, especially when their caregivers sang.

An observational case study of one toddler helps demonstrate how music provides an opportunity for children to use their newly developing physical and motor skills (Suthers 2001). Over a period of time, the toddler went from sucking on wooden sticks to learning how to tap, knock, roll, and clap them. Music also encouraged him to engage in rhythmic movements. At first, when music was played, he asked to be picked up by the caregivers so that he could dance with them. Later, he moved to music by himself, engaging in many different movements such as stamping, crawling, sliding, and jumping. Music gave him an external framework that helped him become more organized in his behavior.

✔ Practice Tip

Using Music to Teach Pre-reading Skills

Chapter 1 provides many ideas on how to use music to promote children's language development and pre-reading skills. The following are three of the best ideas:

Sing Rhyming Songs

The ability to recognize rhyming sounds at age three is a good predictor of later reading ability. We teach this oral language skill largely through song and word play (making up new words that rhyme).

Many common children's songs rhyme, so this is easy. Once children know a song, let them sing the rhyming words without you. They have fun doing this, and it forces them to think about the rhyme.

Sing Songs with Alliteration

Alliteration is the repetition of sounds at the beginning of words. These aren't as common as rhyming songs and chants. Here is one in which you can make up funny words to fit every child's name into the song in a rhyme, as well as emphasizing the alliteration of the letter "w."

Willoughby Wallaby Woo
An elephant sat on you
Willoughby Wallaby Wam
An elephant sat on Sam.

You can substitute a different word for "Wam" to make a rhyme with any child's name, such as "wave" for "Dave."

Clap to the Beat

Another of the key pre-reading skills is syllable segmentation: awareness of where words break into syllables. You can help children learn this by clapping or beating drums on the beat, or even clapping on each word. Conveniently, the beat in some songs breaks between words, sometimes between syllables. Eventually, you can try clapping your hands on each syllable of a song or nursery rhyme, for example, Twin-kle-Twin-kle-lit-tle-star.

Music Promotes Children's Language Development

Research found that babies who experienced more singing and music activities with their teacher-caregivers made more vocalizations than children who had little exposure to music in their early care and education programs (Forrai 1997). Specifically, five- to twelve-month-olds vocalized the most when teacher-caregivers sang to them for extended periods of time. When teacher-caregivers sang for shorter periods with interruptions, babies imitated their mouth movements by making more lip movements, rather than vocalizing.

Music Promotes Pre-reading Skills

Preschoolers who are better in music also tend to be better in other kinds of oral language skills, particularly phonological awareness skills that are a foundation for learning to read (Peynircioglu, Durgunoglu, and Oney-Kusefoglu 2002). This makes sense, because both of these skills—musical and phonological awareness—test the child's ability to recognize different sounds. When the child begins to learn to read, a sensitivity to the sounds within words will help the child to "sound out" new words.

In one study of four- to five-year-olds, those who demonstrated an ability to recognize differences in pitch were also found to score better on reading tests and a phonemic awareness test than children who could not recognize pitch differences (Lamb and Gregory 1993). In this study, children were asked whether two notes or two chords (notes played at the same time) were different from each other. Children were also given two different reading tests. One test measured children's knowledge of print and letter sounds, and their ability to read common words and match one word to another. The second test measured their ability to blend two consonants together and their ability to read nonsense syllables. Finally, children were given a phonemic awareness test that measured their ability to recognize words that had the same beginning sound (alliteration) or ending sound (rhyme). Researchers found that children who did better at recognizing differences between two notes or two chords with different pitches also did better on both reading tests and the phonemic awareness test. Learning to recognize differences between two musical notes may help children hear different sounds in words, a necessary skill when learning to read.

PROMISING PRACTICE

Music Throughout the Day

What We Saw

The teacher walked around the room singing, "Good morning, good morning to you" as children started their activities. Some children hummed along, and some sang "Good morning" to each other.

At cleanup time, the teacher sang "I see [child's name] cleaning up." She used each child's name while singing and clapping a rhythm. She sang and clapped fast, slow, soft, and loud. Cleanup finished quickly and easily.

Before lunch, the teacher used the tune "If you're happy and you know it clap your hands," but inserted her own words: "If you wash your hands and sit down, we'll eat lunch." The children started singing along while following the directions in the song.

What It Means

In some classrooms, music is a part of everyday activity. Children are natural partners in this. Singing directions will often gain the attention and cooperation of children. Music sets a pleasant atmosphere in the classroom. It says to a child, "I am enjoying being here with you, and I show it with my voice."

Music Experiences Promote Math Skills

Researchers were surprised to discover, some years ago, that adult musicians score better on tests of spatial thinking (a math skill) than do other adults (Hassler, Birbaumer, and Fiel 1985). More surprising is that this can be seen even in novice musicians: preschoolers. For example, studies have found that preschoolers who have more music experiences at home do better on tests measuring early math skills (Georghegan and Mitchelmore 1996). Specifically, four- to five-year-olds who more often listened to their own music tapes or CDs at home and who had family members who more often sang to them had better math skills. The math test measured counting skills, addition and subtraction skills, and the ability to recognize differences between more and less.

These findings show us that music and math are connected somehow, but they don't tell us what is causing the connection. To see if music experience *causes* improvements in math reasoning, researchers have conducted experiments. Two studies found that children's participation in musical activities at their early care and education programs caused improvements on tests measuring spatial intelligence (Rauschler et al. 1997; Gromko and Poorman 1998). The spatial intelligence tests used in both of these studies measured things such as children's ability to complete a puzzle and the ability to recognize that two geometric designs are the same.

The first study compared four groups of three- to four-year-olds in preschool classes (Rauschler et al. 1997). Some children received piano keyboard instruction and group singing lessons, others received lessons with computers rather than keyboards, a third group received just group singing lessons, and the fourth group received no special instruction. After six months, the researchers found that the keyboard and group singing instruction group had significantly improved their scores on tests of spatial-temporal reasoning, whereas the other three groups had not shown any significant improvement.

In a second study, researchers compared two groups of children, ages three to four (Gromko and Poorman 1998). The first group participated in a weekly thirty-minute music class at their early care and education program. Each week, a new song was taught to the children. Children were encouraged to sing the song, to move their bodies to the song's rhythm, to play the song by using songbells (similar to a xylophone) or hand chimes, to make a picture of the song by using round stickers, and to feel a sensory chart that portrayed the song's contour (such as showing the differences between higher and lower pitches in the song). Each child's family also received a twenty-note set of songbells to allow children to practice playing new songs at home and a tape of the songs they learned so that children could sing and listen to these songs at home. The second group of children did not receive the music program. After seven months, researchers found that children in the music program significantly improved on the tests of spatial intelligence, while the other children's scores were unchanged.

Most studies finding that musical instruction causes improvements in spatial-mathematical reasoning have been of piano keyboard instruction. Because a keyboard is laid out in a linear sequence, like a number series, this made some sense. But this last study did not include keyboard instruction, but rather singing and other musical experiences. Apparently, all kinds of musical experiences may have an impact on math and spatial reasoning abilities.

This raises the question: why are musical experience and math/spatial reasoning linked together? Recent research on brain functioning offers one possible explanation. Researchers have found that a very similar pattern of brain activity is associated with musical thinking and with spatial-temporal thinking (Leng and Shaw 1991). This could explain why instruction in one could lead to improvement in the other.

What about the Mozart Effect?

Does listening to Mozart raise children's IQs? A lot of people think so. Surprisingly, the research that led to the exaggerated claim of the "Mozart Effect" wasn't about IQ and didn't study young children. It was a study of young adults (college students), which showed that listening to a Mozart sonata improved their performance on a spatial reasoning test if the test was given immediately after listening to Mozart (Rauscher et al. 1993).

Other researchers have tried to reproduce this finding, with little success (Chabris 1999; McKelvie and Low 2002). None of the studies have yet reported results on young children, or on brain development, or with any effects measured for more than a day later.

☑ *Practice Tip*

Integrating Song into the Whole Day

Sing about What You Are Doing

While you prepare a bottle for an infant, sing about what you are doing. Use a tune you know well, and make up your own words. To use an easy example, take "Mary had a little lamb," but sing "Sally had a little bottle, little bottle, little bottle . . . , the milk was white as snow." This will soothe the infant, and probably you too!

Sing about What the Children Are Doing

Singing about the actions and verbalizations of children gives immediate positive feedback to them. This is especially important with infants.

Make Up New Words to a Familiar Melody

Instead of "Row, row, row your boat," try substituting the words "Push, push, push the broom, straight across the floor, first go right, then go left, then go push some more." There are endless possibilities in this. You'll be surprised how much both you and the children enjoy this.

Repeat the Children's Names in Song

When children wake up, sing their names in a soothing way to help them feel safe and secure. "Maria row the boat ashore, hallelujah, Maria waking up on the floor, hallelujah."

As far as we know, there is no Mozart Effect for the development of young children. That so many people believe this rumor is probably due to the enthusiasm of individuals who stand to make money by selling us tapes with titles such as "Build Your Baby's Brain." Not only the public, but also our policy makers have been fooled. The states of Georgia and Tennessee funded programs to give classical music CDs to every new mother in the state! In Florida, child care programs are now required by law to play classical music every day (Shonkoff and Phillips 2000).

Playing classical music in your child care classroom is probably a good idea, but not because it will raise IQ. Some studies have found that calming music helps elementary-aged children do better on school tasks than without music. The same study found that children did worse than normal when listening to arousing and aggressive music (Hallam, Price, and Katsarou 2002). This suggests that music may help children learn by affecting their emotions, either calming them in ways that help them concentrate or arousing them in ways that distract them from learning. In addition, there is nothing special about Mozart, so far as anyone knows. We think the jazz of Count Basie is likely to have just as many benefits for child development.

Music appears to have special promise in helping children who are diagnosed with intellectual or social-emotional disabilities. Soothing background music in a classroom has been found to reduce the activity level of children who are hyperactive and improve the concentration of children who have several kinds of special needs (Crncec, Wilson, and Prior 2006). Several studies have found that systematic music programs improve the classroom motivation and attention, and the social interaction of children diagnosed with an autism spectrum disorder (Wigram and Gold 2006).

Musical Skill Development by Teachers

Some teachers seem to effortlessly capture young children's attention with group-singing activities, while other teachers spend all their time nagging children to sit down and pay attention. Researchers wondered if the skills to create a wonderful group singing time could be taught. They tested a simple training program for teachers and found that it was very effective (Field 1999).

In this study, teachers from five preschools attended a music training program, and teachers from five other preschools did not. The training program provided teachers-caregivers with suggestions for songs and musical activities to use with young children. Demonstrations of these musical activities were also provided to model their use. Finally, other ideas for improving the effectiveness of these activities, such as changing the seating of children or using visual materials, were suggested after observing teachers in their classrooms. After six training sessions over a period of four months, children whose teachers had received the music training had become significantly more attentive during group singing times than children whose teachers had not received this training.

Some teachers are uncomfortable singing with children or feel they don't have the expertise needed to plan musical activities. This research shows that teachers can learn (from special classes or workshops) how to plan and implement musical activities that effectively capture children's interest. Even if these classes are not available, any teacher can learn by observing others who are good with music activities.

PROMISING PRACTICE

Moving to the Beat

What We Saw

The teacher starts playing music on a tape player during free-choice time. Four toddlers, hearing the music, rush over to the tape player. They gather on the rug and start dancing to the music. The teacher watches for a moment, then provides a basket of scarves. The children wave the scarves around while dancing, and the teacher shows them how to match their movements to the tempo of the music. Another teacher brings out some instruments, and the children experiment using cymbals, shakers, and tambourines. Some are able to match the beat of the music; others are not. But they all laugh together.

What It Means

All early childhood programs can make music and movement activities a normal part of their classrooms. Movement to music helps develop coordination, gross-motor skills, and self-regulation of behavior. It also gives children an opportunity to creatively express themselves. Creative expression, in this case, means using movement to express feelings or ideas. Adding props such as scarves and instruments gives children more ways to experience how they can match their actions to the rhythm or mood of the music.

Restricted Music

What We Saw

Musical instruments (triangles, rhythm sticks, maracas, sandpaper blocks) are kept in a lidded plastic bin on a high shelf above the puzzles. The children cannot reach the bin. When they ask a teacher if they can play with the musical instruments, she says, "Maybe later." (When we talk with her later, she says the instruments make the room too loud during free playtime.)

What Would Work Better

Instead of being a special activity that is done only at special times, with a teacher's assistance, music should be freely available, a part of the whole day. Like other core topics (language learning, math, science, self-regulation), music learning can be integrated into other activities. But this will happen more easily if musical instruments are available where children can choose to use them independently. Music learning is also more likely to occur, and the music corner is less likely to get wild, if the teacher encourages free choice and the proper use of instruments.

A music area can be set up in every classroom. It can nicely tie in with dramatic play, blocks, or science. This area could contain items such as the following:

- Musical instruments, preferably real instruments
- Books with pictures showing musical instruments and people playing music in other cultures
- A sturdy tape player or two, with favorite tapes
- Tapes for children to use in recording themselves
- Dancing wands, scarves, and costumes
- Song charts with familiar songs and fingerplays

Using Recorded Music at Naptime

Would you like more planning time? Then play music at naptime! One notable researcher conducted a brief study to investigate whether playing classical guitar music at naptime would help toddlers and preschoolers fall asleep faster (Field 1999). One toddler classroom and one preschool classroom were observed for four days during naptime. Classical guitar music during naptime and no music during naptime were alternated every other day. The results indicated that both toddlers and preschoolers fell asleep significantly faster on the days when the classical guitar music was played than when it was not played. Toddlers fell asleep an average of nine minutes faster with music than without. Preschoolers fell asleep an average of eight minutes faster with music than without. (Don't tell the guitar players that their music puts children to sleep.)

Conclusion

Children have a special interest in music. As we have seen, even babies are adept listeners of music. Toddlers and preschoolers gradually become better listeners and singers as their musical abilities develop. Music experiences in early childhood both at home and at their early care and education programs help children to feel comfortable listening to music and learning about it. Early childhood teachers play a crucial role in the attitudes and confidence of children toward music and in the development of early skills that predict later musical abilities.

Musical skill and appreciation are worthy goals on their own, but they also contribute to children's physical, social, and academic development. Children who have more opportunities to sing, participate in creative movement, play musical instruments, and listen to music will not only have better musical skills, but will also have greater opportunities to practice new physical skills. Children's academic skills in the areas of language, reading, and math will also be promoted by these musical activities.

Further Reading

On Research

Journal of Research on Music Education

Music Education Journal

On Practice

Achilles, E. 1999. Creating music environments in early childhood programs. *Young Children* 54 (1): 21–26.

Andres, B. 1991. From research to practice: Preschool children and their movement responses to music. *Young Children* 46 (11): 22–27.

Dowell, R. I. 1995. *Mother Ruth's rhymes: Lyrical finger plays and action verses for fun reinforcement of concepts across the curriculum.* Terre Haute, IN: Pollyanna Productions.

Jalongo, M. R. 1996. Using recorded music with young children: A guide for nonmusicians. *Young Children* 51 (5): 6–14.

Moomaw, S. 1997. *More than singing: Discovering music in preschool and kindergarten.* Saint Paul, MN: Redleaf Press.

Ringgenberg, S. 2003. Music as a teaching tool: Creating story songs. *Young Children* 58 (5): 76–79.

Silberg, J. 1998. *I can't sing book: For grownups who can't carry a tune in a paper bag.* Beltsville, MD: Gryphon House.

Silberg, J., and P. Schiller. 2002. *The complete book of rhymes, songs, poems, fingerplays, and chants.* Beltsville, MD: Gryphon House.

Wolf, J. 1994. Singing with children is a cinch! *Young Children* 49 (4): 20–25.

Children's Books

Dowell, R. I. 1987. *Move over Mother Goose!* Beltsville, MD: Gryphon House.

Frazee, M. 1999. *Hush, little baby: A folk song with pictures.* San Diego: Harcourt Brace.

Guthrie, W. 1998. *This land is your land.* Boston: Little, Brown and Co.

Haber, J. Z. 1990. *This old man.* New York: Macmillan.

Hale, S. J. 1984. *Mary had a little lamb*. New York: Holiday House.

Hoberman, M. A. 2000. *The eensy-weensy spider*. Boston: Little, Brown and Co.

Kantz, R. M. 1988. *This old man: Counting song*. New York: Dodd, Mead and Co.

Kellogg, S. 1998. *A-hunting we will go!* New York: Morrow Junior Books.

Kovalski, M. 1987. *The wheels on the bus*. Boston: Little, Brown and Co.

La Prise, L. 1997. *The hokey pokey*. New York: Simon & Schuster.

Quackenbush, R. 1973. *Go tell aunt Rhody*. Philadelphia: Lippincott.

Schiller, P., and T. Moore. 1993. *Where is Thumpkin?* Beltsville, MD: Gryphon House.

Other Resources

Playing CDs is the easiest way to learn new songs. There are too many great ones to even begin a list. Bookstores, music stores, and early childhood supply houses will carry a wide selection, and you can find music to fit your own taste.

The National Association for Music Education has an early childhood section on their Web site with a good list of resources at www.menc.org/.

The Early Childhood Music and Movement Association is a terrific group with good resources. You can contact them at www.ecmma.org/ or at:

ECMMA
10691 Livingston Dr.
Northglenn, CO 80234
303-447-8986

~~~~~~~~~~~~~~~~~~~~~~~~~~~~~~~~~~~~~

When Teachers Reflect: *Singing as an Instinct*

Every known culture has its own lullabies for babies, and babies everywhere respond more positively to the songs we sing to them than to other music.

Most behaviors that are universal (all humans do them) and species-specific (only humans do them) are likely to have a biological base. In other words, we probably have some human instincts for singing lullabies.

This may be why singing a lullaby to a baby feels so right. It takes a powerful opposing force to override our instinct to croon to the little ones in our company.

Think about it: what makes us refrain from singing? Our own shyness about singing in front of others can put a damper on us. So can the setting in which we work. Some classrooms, if they have adopted a highly professionalized, school-like setting, can make you feel awkward singing, much as you would feel inappropriate if you broke into song while in line at the bank. But the research evidence suggests that to *refrain* from song is unnatural, while singing to young children is the human thing to do.

~~~~~~~~~~~~~~~~~~~~~~~~~~~~~~~~~~~~~

When Teachers Reflect: *Singing May Be Good for Teachers Too*

This chapter summarized the research showing that young children love music and that music is good for them. Could the same be true for teachers?

Have you noticed that singing to children puts you in a better mood? Do you smile more when you sing?

Perhaps song makes for a better workplace for adults. If true, we suspect that, just as with children, music that we make ourselves (with our own voices and instruments) has a more powerful and positive effect on us than does recorded music to which we listen.

Letter to Parents

Music and Song in Our Classroom

We do a lot with music in our early childhood program. We have simple musical instruments for the children, we play and listen to music, and we seem to sing all day long. We do this for three good reasons:

1. Music is fun! The children (and we teachers) love to sing and make music.

2. Children who have more experience with music at this age will have greater interest and ability with music later. These early childhood years lay a foundation for the future.

3. Early experiences with music also predict better language and math learning.

We teach pre-reading skills with music. Preschool children who have more music in their programs tend to do better on tests of early arithmetic skills. We hope to expose the children to many kinds of music this year.

If your family has some special music (on CDs or tapes) you would like to loan to our class, please let us know. If you play an instrument, would you like to play for the children in our class sometime?

From *Intellectual Development: Connecting Science and Practice in Early Childhood Settings* (Redleaf Press, 2009).

Why We Scribble and Paint

The Development of Artistic Expression

Charlie's dad has just arrived, and Charlie rushes him over to the art center. Charlie points to his drawing on the wall. "Look Dad!" he exclaims. "I drew the monkey we saw at the zoo!" Charlie's dad admires the drawing and about parts of it asks, "What is this?" Kasha, who is busily painting at the easel, turns around eagerly and announces that she is using pink paint. Meanwhile, Rogelio asks the teacher, Marissa, one of the caregivers in the four-year-old room, to help him staple his drawings together to create a book for his mom.

Young children have enthusiasm for art, and their interest starts very early in their lives. Artistic expression is a good thing in its own right as a way for children to express their creativity and represent their daily thoughts and experiences. Art also helps promote children's development in other areas. For example, children who excel in drawing also tend to develop larger vocabularies and better literacy skills (Fast 1997; Toomela 2002). In this chapter, after briefly describing the stages of drawing and artistic drawing development in early childhood, we discuss how teachers-caregivers can support children's artistic creativity, their development of drawing skills, and their appreciation of art. Early care and education programs can provide excellent opportunities for children to experiment with and appreciate art.

Children's Understanding of Drawings

Our modern world is filled with pictures, not just in picture books but also on road signs, food packages, newspapers, TVs, and so forth. As adults, we are constantly viewing pictures and symbols and then translating or interpreting their meaning. As a result, we can forget the difficult mental task we perform in order to understand what they mean. Unlike the things we see in the real world, pictures are usually small, flat (two-dimensional), and lacking color, compared to the things the pictures represent. Despite these differences, young children need no instruction to understand a picture. For example, in one of the first demonstrations of this ability, researchers studied a two-year-old who had never before seen a flat picture of any object and found that he could easily tell them what object each picture showed (Hochberg and Brooks 1962). Researchers also have found that one-year-olds respond in the same manner to real objects and their pictures. This indicates their clear understanding of what the picture represents (Winner 2006).

This raises an interesting question: if infants and toddlers understand the "sameness" of an object and its picture, do they also understand how they are different? Surprisingly, until about age three, many children actually confuse the object and picture, acting as if the picture were real (Beilin and Pearlman 1991). For example, a two-year-old may shake a picture of a rattle and expect it to make noise. Children can become frightened of a picture of a bee in a picture book, thinking it might sting them. They act as if the picture can do the things the real object can do.

Children under age two and a half or three do not understand that the picture is not just a separate object, but also *represents* another object. In one experiment, toddlers were asked to drop colored balls down a tube. An adult instructed the children which ball to drop by using a picture of the ball. Two-year-olds couldn't match the picture to the correct ball. In fact, some children even tried to stuff the picture of the ball down the tube, showing that they treated the pictures as objects (Callaghan 2000).

At this young age, children commonly have difficulty holding in mind, at the same time, two different ideas about the same object (Flavell 1988). For example, presented with a picture of a piece of candy, children can think of the picture as an object (a colored picture on paper) or as a symbol of an object (candy), but they are just beginning to gain the ability to think about it in both ways at once. Until about age four, children sometimes still make mistakes in interpreting the meaning of a picture. (Will it taste good if I eat it?)

EXPOSING INFANTS AND TODDLERS TO ART EXPERIENCES

- Infants learn through observation and imitation. Provide prints or images of fine art by a variety of artists for babies to look at. Post only a few at a time on walls (or ceilings) where infants can see them when lying on the floor, seated in your lap, in exersaucers, or in infant seats.

- Provide younger infants with materials that allow them to practice movements and see the results—water to splash in, sand to wiggle their toes in and squish and smooth with their fingers, applesauce or other foods to smear around on the high-chair tray, "pat mats" filled with water and plastic shapes that jiggle and move when the child touches and squeezes it.

- Provide older infants with basic art materials, such as the following:
  - fat crayons that are easy to hold, washable markers, paintbrushes with nontoxic paint
  - large paper for drawing—with enough space for the big arm movements of beginning artists (at least twelve by eighteen inches and placed wide side toward child for the predominantly side-to-side motions that are made with the whole arm)

- Model the kind of movements the infant is capable of doing: the horizontal arc (side-to-side), vertical arc (dot-dot-dot), and push pull (top to bottom). Add some new movements and encourage the child to copy you. But be sure to stay within the child's "zone of proximal development"—what the child is capable of imitating (more on this in the next chapter).

- Talk about the child's actions and what is happening on the paper. "You moved your arm side to side and made wide green lines on the paper." "Dot, dot, dot—listen to the sound you're making with your little dots all over!"

- Describe the emotions you see the child expressing and the emotional response you have to a child's art. "You seemed excited when you moved the paintbrush up and down so fast on your painting." "The colors in your picture remind me of a sad, rainy day."

Children's Drawing Development

Drawing is one of the most common and popular art activities among young children. It is also an activity that is adaptable to a variety of mediums. Children can draw with a variety of tools, including crayons, colored pencils, markers, fingerpaint, paintbrushes, and chalk. Researchers have found that children generally proceed through predictable stages of drawing development (Herberholz and Hanson 1995), but some children may progress through these stages more quickly than others.

1. Artistic Development in Infancy

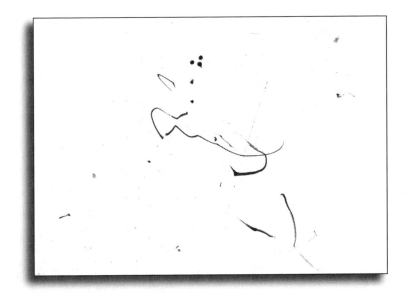

Random scribbling, age twelve-and-a-half months

You might be surprised to learn that drawing skills actually begin to develop during infancy. Imagine a two-month-old baby lying on his back on the changing table. He might be kicking his legs and moving his arms in the air while waiting to get his diaper changed. At this age, children are just beginning to notice these movements. These patterns in the air could be considered children's first drawings (Bleiker 1999).

Later, when infants are between four and five months old, they learn how to hold objects in their hands. At this age, babies often experiment with hitting objects against each other or against the floor. Through this exploration, they are learning the skills necessary to use a drawing instrument, such as a crayon or paintbrush (Herberholz and Hanson 1995).

2. Random Scribbling

Starting at around one year old, children begin to make their first drawings on paper. Up through about age two, children explore their ability

Random scribbling, age eighteen months

to make marks on something where marks did not previously exist (such as a blank sheet of paper). At this age, children exercise little control over the marks they make. Instead, they experiment with moving their arm and hand in different ways (Colbert 1997; Herberholz and Hanson 1995).

☑ *Practice Tip*

Working with Toddlers

Toddlers are just beginning to master small-motor movements, so be sure to provide chunky crayons and large-handled paint-brushes that are easily held in little hands. Broken pieces of crayons can be melted in a muffin tin, and when they dry, they become circular crayons that are easy to hold for this age child. Do not let the crayon pieces melt until they become one drab color; stop just when they take the shape of the tin. It does not matter if the colors are mixed because children delight in seeing the colors change as they draw across the paper.

COMMENTING ON CHILDREN'S ART

When a toddler brings you a "controlled scribbles" drawing, you might describe the picture for the child. "I see you used blue and yellow paint in this picture." An accurate, objective description gives voice to the child's experience, and this works with any age child.

When a toddler is approaching "named scribbling," you can also name the things you imagine seeing in the picture, much as you might name the different things you see represented by clouds. This helps children learn that their pictures can represent objects in the world, helping them make the transition to symbolic (representational) drawings.

However, when a preschooler (age three or older) brings you a completed drawing, be cautious about naming the picture for the child. "Oh, I see you drew a dog," might result in a hurt look because the child thought she drew a horse. Instead, ask the child to describe the drawing. Let the child be your guide in interpreting the drawing.

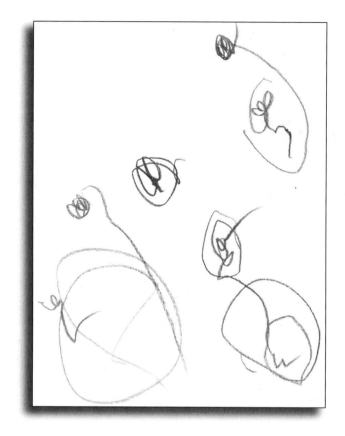

Controlled scribbling, repeats certain shapes, age twenty months

3. Controlled Scribbling

After toddlers engage in random scribbling for approximately six months, they enter a new stage of drawing development called controlled scribbling (Herberholz and Hanson 1995). Drawings may continue to look very similar to those that children make when they are scribbling randomly, but during this stage, children begin to realize that they can determine how the marks appear on the page. They may repeatedly make the marks that they most enjoy. New movements may also begin to appear, such as rotational marks made with circular motions and vertical and horizontal lines (Mathews 1994).

One researcher concluded that toddlers start with simple scribbles, then begin to combine those simple marks into combinations that are more complex (Kellogg 1969). For example, a toddler might add a vertical line to a horizontal line, making a cross, and then draw a circle around that to make a mandala. After much practice with these controlled scribbles, and having adults try to see things in the scribbles, children may get the idea that their drawings *represent* something. The scribbles might still be meaningless at this point (not intended by the child to represent anything), but if the adult says, "this looks like a person" or "that looks like a house," the child begins to get the idea to represent something when drawing.

At this stage, children may also begin to draw and describe the movement of something, a drawing known as an action representation (Matthews 1994). Children usually use their earliest drawings to represent verbs, rather than nouns. The drawing is about portraying the movement of an object, rather than the object itself. For example, one two-year-old was observed saying, "It's going round the corner. It's going round the corner . . . it's gone now" while painting (Matthews 1994: 5). He was describing the movement of his paintbrush, rather than describing what the painting looked like. Two and a half months later, the same two-year-old said, "This is an airplane," while painting using rotational movements (Matthews 1994: 10). Instead of painting something that looked like an airplane, the toddler was imagining the movement of an airplane in the air with his paintbrush. Finally, a three-year-old was observed using circular movements while painting. When the researcher asked him about his painting, he said that he was "washing cups" and later said that he was "washing a car" (Matthews 1994: 41).

4. Named Scribbling

Children approximately three years old begin to name their drawings (Herberholz and Hanson 1995). The actual appearance of these drawings continues to be similar to those made during the random and controlled scribbling stages, but at this stage children begin to understand that their drawings can represent things they see and experience in their lives. Children usually name a picture only after they have finished drawing it. In other words, children may begin with the intention of drawing something particular, such as their dog or their mom. However, the finished product may be called something entirely different, depending on what the drawing looks like to the child. The next day, the child may even give the same drawing a different name.

Named scribbling, "A dragon in a castle," age three-and-a-half years

Creating Art Time for the Older Children

What We Saw

The classroom has a mixed age group from birth to age three years. During certain times of the day, the younger children sleep longer than the older ones. During these times, a student teacher or float person is often available. The teachers have decided this would be a perfect time to create individual art experiences for children. The teachers have prepared an area near a sink by covering a low table with newspapers and have gathered smocks and art supplies. The teachers usually provide a snack before a child engages in art exploration. Then, as the opportunity arises, one or two children can be at the table exploring a variety of art materials. After the children explore art media, the teachers put the artwork up to dry and later display it in the room.

What It Means

The teachers understand the developmental level of the children in their classroom. Large group art projects will not be successful with infants and toddlers because their attention span is short and their need for adult interaction is high. By carefully looking at their daily schedule, they were able to carve out time to make art a relaxing and individual experience for the older children. They have paid special attention to the environment by making sure they were near a sink and had all the supplies available. They also understood that young children are less likely to put art supplies in their mouth if their tummies are full! Finally, they understand how important it is for children to see their creations displayed.

5. Early Symbolic Stage

Beginning at around three years old, children learn to make symbols that can represent people and objects (Herberholz and Hanson 1995). One of the first shapes they learn to draw is a circle (as we noted in chapter 2). A circle can be used to represent many different objects. For example, children's first attempts to draw a person usually consist of a circle, often with eyes in it, and with straight lines sticking out to represent arms and legs (but no body yet!). This symbol is referred to as a "tadpole" figure. Beginning at around age three, children all over the world make this same tadpole figure when asked to draw a person (Cox and Parkin 1986).

Children begin drawing people's bodies later than heads, arms, and legs. Unlike heads, legs, and arms, bodies cannot be drawn by using natural shapes such as circles and straight lines. As a result, they are more difficult to conceptualize. Researchers have observed three major ways that children begin to draw bodies (Matthews 1994). Some children may draw bodies by using patches of color that do not have a distinct shape. Later, they become more skilled at using lines to represent the contours of the body. Other children begin to represent the body by coloring the space between the two leg lines in their tadpole figure or by drawing a horizontal line between the ends of the leg lines. A square or rectangle is added to represent the body, and two more leg lines are drawn below it. Finally, children may also draw a U-shape underneath the head and attach legs to the rounded bottom section.

Early symbolic stage, tadpole people, age three-and-a-half years

The inaccuracies of the tadpole drawings of humans are not due to children's lack of knowledge about the human form, but appear to be caused by lack of planning, effort, or skill in making the drawing. This is shown by an experiment in which a researcher began by asking children to simply draw a person, and then asked more specific questions (Cox and Parkin 1986). The three-year-olds in this study began by drawing tadpole figures, but when asked to draw a person with a tummy, the next picture included a torso between the head and legs. When asked to draw a person holding a flower, the following picture would often include an arm with a flower on the end. In another experiment, when the adult asked the preschooler to name the body parts needed to draw a person, the children were then far more likely to include details such as arms and a torso in their drawings (Golomb and Farmer 1983). These studies show how difficult the drawing task is for young children, and they also show how much better young children can perform when stimulated and prodded by teachers. By asking children about their drawings, adults

✔️ *Practice Tip*

Adding to the Art Activity

Become an active participant in the children's art activities. Keep art materials available during free play. Make suggestions to get children started, or stimulate them with a provocative question. "I wonder what kind of house a monkey would build? Can anyone draw one?" As children begin to paint or color, ask them about their work. Identify the colors they are using. Ask them what they are drawing. If possible, take notes on what the children tell you. Ask if you can write down what they say on the paper after their project is completed. In this way, parents can enjoy the picture and discuss it with the child. The art is also a pre-reading exercise because children see you write the words they said.

may help children conceptualize something they might not have had in mind, even though they had experienced it.

COMMUNICATING THROUGH ART

Children often draw things that come directly from their own life experiences. Look for opportunities to learn about the children through a discussion of their art projects. If a child shares with you that the girl in her picture is crying, ask her why the child is crying. The child may be trying to represent something sad that happened to her, and your question will give her the chance to express her feelings. Clinical psychologists use art to help children express and understand their emotions.

6. Late Symbolic Stage

During the early symbolic stage of the preschool years, the placement of drawings on a page is rather random, with symbols for people, animals, houses, and other common objects seeming to float in space. Later, a ground line appears, often shown by drawing green blades of grass and

Late symbolic stage, with many details (toes, fingers, ears, glasses) and the word "Grandpa" written on the top, age six years and ten months

shading the top half of the paper blue, to indicate the sky (Bleiker 1999). During this stage, children's symbols also become more complex and detailed. After children learn to draw a body along with the arms and legs, they begin to add more details such as feet, hands, fingers, a nose, lips, teeth, clothing, hair, and eyelashes (Herberholz and Hanson 1995; Bleiker 1999).

By the age of six, children will often exaggerate or make certain parts of their drawing more detailed in order to reflect their lived experiences (Herberholz and Hanson 1995). For example, if a child just received a new hat for her birthday, she might draw her head bigger to emphasize her new hat. Similarly, a child who has just broken his arm might draw his arm and fingers with more detail.

Table 4.1: Stages in Drawing (Herberholz and Hanson 1995)

Developmental stages of drawing	Age	Characteristics
Infancy	4 months–1 year	• Notices movements of arms and legs • Learns to grasp objects and strike them against each other or against the floor
Random Scribbling	1–2 years	• Learns to make marks on paper • Uses three basic movements: horizontal arc, vertical arc, and push pull
Controlled Scribbling	2–3 years	• Learns to make marks more deliberately • Makes horizontal lines, vertical lines, and rotational movements • Draws "action representations"
Named Scribbling	3–4 years	• Learns that drawings can represent the things in their environments • Names the objects in drawings both before and after the drawing is finished
Early Symbolic Stage	4–5 years	• Learns to make symbols to represent people ("tadpole" figure) and other familiar objects • Later adds a "body" to the tadpole figure
Late Symbolic Stage	5–6 years	• Adds a ground line and sky to drawings to help relate objects to each other • Adds more detail to common symbols, such as eyelashes and lips to people • Exaggerates or provides more detail to emphasize lived experiences

Drawing Development Is Related to Language and Reading Skills

Children with Better Drawing Skills Have Larger Vocabularies

Research shows that vocabulary skills and drawing skills tend to develop together: when children are better at one, they tend to also be better at the other. In one study, two- to five-year-olds who had a larger vocabulary, who knew more words to describe object characteristics ("rectangle," "green") or relationships between objects ("above," "between"), and who could commit more words to memory were also better at mentally rotating a picture (Toomela 2002). Children who were better at mentally rotating pictures (who could identify the same picture when it was rotated) also drew more detailed pictures that were of higher quality.

The researcher proposed that knowing the names for more objects may help children notice details and attend to these details when they are drawing. To illustrate, he gave the example of a child who had learned the words "poodle" and "collie." Before learning these words, this child probably drew all dogs similarly. Now, the child would likely pay more attention to the differences between collies and poodles and might try to draw these two dogs differently. Of course, the opposite effect may also be true. Children who experiment with drawing poodles and collies may be more likely to remember the names for these dogs. When a child acts upon an object (in this case, by drawing it), this probably reinforces the word for that object.

PROMISING PRACTICE

Communicating with Pictures and Words

What We Saw

Preschoolers sit at tables, drawing pictures in their own personal journals. As they finish, the teachers talk to each child, listening carefully and making eye contact, while the child explains what is happening in their picture. The teachers write down the explanations each child provides underneath each picture. One child describes his picture, saying, "That is me. I am a people. I have legs and I like my hands."

What It Means

Providing a journal activity for older preschoolers is an excellent way to increase art awareness and literacy skills. The teachers encouraged imagination in the children by letting them draw whatever they desired and then, through thoughtful questions, helped the children tell a story about their picture. Teachers were also able to get a mental snapshot (assessment) of each child's level of art and literacy development through this journal activity.

Children with Better Drawing Skills Also Have Better Preliteracy Skills

Research has found that kindergarten children's preliteracy skills are related to their drawing abilities. In one study, two- to four-year-olds were asked to both draw and write (Levin and Bus 2003). When asked to write, children printed writing-like symbols that began to look like letters as the children got older. At first, children think of letters as just other objects that can be drawn. As they get older, children slowly begin to think of their writing as different from their other drawings. Regardless of their age, when children's drawing skills were better, their letter-printing was also better. This study suggests that drawing pictures is a form of communication that precedes writing letters and words, and writing letters derives from general drawing ability.

In another study, children were asked to draw a picture of themselves and their teachers. Their teachers rated the children's readiness to learn to read (Fast 1997). Children with more advanced drawing skills were found to be better prepared to begin to read, according to their teachers. We aren't sure if teaching drawing will help children with their reading. It is possible, for example, that some families provide more stimulation to their children in general, including both preliteracy and artistic opportunities. But it is also possible that literacy and drawing skills help support each other. Just as reading requires the recognition that print has a purpose, beginning artists learn that drawing can tell a story. Children who become skillful in one of these areas of visual communication will most likely be more skillful in the other as a result.

Avoiding Messy Problems by Limiting Art

What We Saw

The teachers in the three-year-old classroom have decided to put the crayons and markers up on a high shelf and get them out only when they have planned an art activity. They decided to do this after one of the children colored on a shelf. One teacher is also worried that the children will eat the crayons.

Why We See This Mistaken Practice

It is true that children learn through their senses. And, yes, children will taste a crayon. Art may be about exploration, but every classroom will have its limits about what is allowed.

What Would Work Better

Our job as teachers is to help children understand how materials are used correctly. By putting the crayons out of reach, the teachers are not helping the children to learn. Introducing children to one art material at a time, and in small groups or even individually, helps them get the idea of how to use the materials creatively but also competently and appropriately, within classroom limits. Once children know how to use art materials, the materials can be freely available to the children with only a small amount of monitoring by teachers.

Promoting Artistic Development in Early Care and Education Programs

How should early care and education programs implement art activities to best promote children's artistic development? Should teachers focus on the art process or the art product? Should teachers provide direction with art projects or use a hands-off approach? These questions are often debated in the early childhood field and are not easily answered by research. However, consensus exists among art and early childhood educators about the overall goals of a developmentally appropriate early care and education art program.

Art Activities Should Allow Children to Explore Their Own Individuality and Creativity

Art educators and early childhood educators generally agree that art should be meaningful for each individual child (Kellman 1994; Wiedner 1998). In other words, each child should be able to explore and create his or her own meaning, no matter if the art project was planned by the teacher or was entirely child-initiated. For example, art can provide children a way to understand and represent their own experiences if they are provided with the opportunity to individualize art projects. One art educator describes the drawing of a five-year-old girl that depicts a giraffe giving birth to a baby giraffe (Wiedner 1998). The preschooler drew this picture shortly after her mother had given birth to her baby sister, so the drawing represents the child's experience in her family and has personal meaning for her. Two other art educators describe a preschooler's drawings on topics that he had read about, such as a volcano eruption, or of his experiences, such as a flight to Ohio to visit his grandparents (Hanes and Weisman 2000).

SUPPORTING CHILDREN'S INTEREST IN ART

- Mat children's artwork for display in the classroom. Easy mats can be made with contrasting colored paper. The borders make the pictures look special.

- Save old magazines to bring to the classroom to make collages. Children can cut or tear pictures to assemble into collages. The teacher could suggest a theme, perhaps people or animals, or let the children select a theme for themselves. Scraps of ribbon, material, and yarn can also be used to make three-dimensional pictures.

- Almost any good children's book can be used to set the stage for an art activity. Each year, books with superior artwork are awarded the Caldecott Medal. You can get a list of the winners from most libraries or the internet. Brainstorm art ideas after reading a book. For example, *Where the Wild Things Are* is a former Caldecott winner. The young boy in the story sails to a magical land filled with wild things. Children could be asked to create their own wild thing.

With paint, paper, and yarn for hair, there is no way of knowing what the children will create.

♦ Put a sheet of white paper inside an overturned box top. Let a child put dollops of paint on the paper. Then put several marbles in the box, and have the child move the marbles across the paper, by tipping the box, and moving it side to side. The marbles make paths in the paint, creating intersecting patterns. Children see the moving object doing the painting. Small cars (instead of marbles) also make interesting marks. You might ask the children what other objects would work.

♦ Attach a circular piece of paper to the turntable of an old record player. Turn on the player, and give children markers to hold against the paper as it spins. By varying movement of the marker, the children create different lined patterns. Let them use different colors and different thicknesses of markers. Children enjoy that the paper is shaped in a circle, instead of a square or rectangle. The children can also change the speed of the player and see how that affects the drawing. The activity can be expanded by having the children sit on large circular pieces of paper and drawing in all directions by turning around like the turntable.

Teachers-Caregivers Provide Individual Support for Children's Artistic Endeavors

Art teachers and early childhood educators continue to debate the best ways to talk to children about their art. Some have advocated for very little adult conversation so as not to interrupt children's creative processes (Kellogg 1970). Generally, though, educators agree that children benefit from adults who are interested in their artwork (Thompson 1990). Some educators recommend that adults tailor their comments to the child's stage of artistic development and be as specific as possible (Sparling and Sparling 1981). For example, when children are first beginning to draw, teachers might help them notice their drawing movements, the shapes and lines they create, and the colors they choose. Later, when children begin to name their drawings, teachers should listen and talk about the meaning the artwork has for children.

Educators also generally believe that teachers should support, rather than direct, children's art. The support that teachers provide to children will vary depending on each child's needs. For example, one early childhood educator describes a teacher's interaction with two different children (Kolbe 1993). For the first child, the teacher was primarily the listener as the child told a story about her clay snake. The teacher also acted as a facilitator in order to help the child keep the tail from falling off her clay mouse. For the second child, the teacher appreciated and encouraged the increasing details that the child added to her clay crocodiles.

Research confirms that the mere presence of teachers in the art center, with minimal direct interaction with children, is enough to increase children's constructive or dramatic play with art (Kontos and Keyes 1999). In this study, the probability of three- to five-year-old children's constructive or dramatic play with art was three times more likely for an individual child and five times more likely for a small group of children when teachers were present in the art area.

Teachers can also provide support to children's art by being aware of children's current interests and providing the materials and guidance necessary for children to explore these interests. For example, one early childhood educator describes supplying black and white painted cardboard grocery boxes because of children's interest in creating a house structure (Kolbe 1993). The children were given the opportunity to freely transform these three-dimensional materials while the teacher's role was primarily that of an audience who was interested in observing the children's new creations.

PROMISING PRACTICE

Facilitating an Art Corner

What We Saw

The teacher pours paint into the cups at the easel and places a brush in each cup. She helps the child put on a painting smock and writes his name on the paper. Throughout the morning, she helps children take turns painting at the easel, hanging their paintings to dry on a nearby rack. The teacher moves throughout the room but always keeps an eye on the easel, keeping track of the children who asked to paint and offering them a turn when another child finishes. Many children make circular patterns, large and small. One boy carefully makes parallel downward strokes across the page in alternating colors. All children seem to want to fill up the paper and stop when that is accomplished to their satisfaction.

What It Means

The teachers have created a classroom in which every child gets a turn to paint, yet each child is given the time to explore with paint and brushes on his own. The teachers act as facilitators for the creative process, rather than directing it. The children in this classroom do not need the teachers to give them ideas to paint; they have differing ideas of their own! No one feels pressured to hurry up and create. (The teachers and children value the process of making art, not just the end product.) This is made possible because the children waiting their turn to paint are patient. From past experience in this room, they know their turn will come. The teacher monitors the painting easel from across the room, easing the transitions into and out of this area, giving it a small amount of attention across the entire morning.

Teachers-Caregivers Can Encourage the Development of Advanced Drawing Skills

Research shows that children's drawing abilities develop better under certain conditions. One research study investigated whether children's depiction of gender and age in their drawings would vary depending on the circumstances under which they were drawn (Sitten and Light 1992). One group of children in the study were simply asked to draw pictures of a man, woman, boy, and girl. A second group of children were put into pairs and told they were going to play a game. Each pair drew pictures at a table with a divider between them. After drawing pictures of a man, woman, boy, and girl, the children were told to exchange their work with each other and try to guess who was who in the picture. The children then were given a second chance to play the game, to try to improve their drawings. All of the children's drawings were later given to two independent adult judges, in matched pairs of drawings that represented gender and age differences (man/woman, boy/girl, man/boy, woman/girl). Judges were asked to determine who was in each drawing—a man, woman, boy, or girl.

The researchers found that neither group of four-year-olds was significantly better at making gender and age identifiable in their drawings. For the five-year-olds, however, gender differences were more identifiable for the children playing the guessing game with another child than for those who were not. Finally, both the gender and age differences for six-year-olds' drawings were significantly easier to identify for drawings made during the guessing game than for drawings made on their own.

Therefore, the availability of an audience to look at and guess the objects in their drawings may help five- and six-year-olds learn to include details to make their drawings more understandable. The feedback the children received on their first drawings, and the chance to try drawing them better a second time, seemed to make a difference. Teachers might create this kind of audience feedback in their classrooms by encouraging informal discussions between children about their drawings, and also by adding their own comments about the child's drawing. At the same time, the researchers suggest that children may benefit from seeing how someone incorrectly makes conclusions about their drawings. This experience may allow children to get ideas about how to add more detail to their drawings to prevent the same misinterpretations in the future.

Linking Visual and Written Communication

What We Saw

Brad, a preschooler, brings a picture to the teacher. She asks what he drew. Brad says, "It's the Easter Bunny, and he wants to give people presents like Santa." She answers saying, "I can see he has presents in his hands. What will Santa think about a bunny bringing presents?" Brad says, "I'll show you what he thinks," and walks back to the art table. Several minutes later, he approaches the teacher with another picture. She smiles and Brad says, "Look how Santa feels." She looks at the picture and says, "Oh my, Santa looks like he's stuck in the chimney." "See," says Brad, "he can't deliver the presents anyway. He's stuck." She replies, saying, "It's a good thing he has the bunny to help." "I think so too," answers Brad.

What It Means

The teacher begins by asking Brad to interpret his picture, often a good idea with preschoolers. Then, by asking an unexpected question ("What will Santa think?"), this teacher inspired Brad to draw another picture. He was excited to be able to communicate his answer visually. She could have added to this activity by asking Brad if she could write down what he said as a story on the picture. Writing and drawing are two communication systems and, in fact, children who are better at drawing tend to have better preliteracy skills as well.

―――――

Promoting and Maintaining Children's Interest in Making Art

Does the way we encourage art activities in early care and education programs affect children's interest in art? Several researchers have found that how we motivate children to participate in art affects not only children's interest in art, but also the quality of their artwork (Greene and Lepper 1974; Loveland and Oiley 1979). In fact, the studies show us how we might discourage a child's interest in doing artwork if we aren't careful.

In these studies, researchers told one group of preschoolers they would receive a "good-player award," a ribbon with their name, school, and a gold star attached, if they participated in drawing activities (using large markers on sheets of paper). A second group of preschoolers were asked if they would like to draw pictures for the researchers, but were told nothing about a reward for the drawings. All the children had been observed the week before, and the week after, to see how much drawing they would choose to do if it was a free-choice activity in the classroom.

For the children who normally didn't choose to do drawing, the offer of a reward helped. Those who were told they would get a reward for drawing produced more drawings. They also produced more drawings on their own a week later, showing they had learned to be more interested in drawing.

The children who normally chose drawing as an activity also made more drawings when they were rewarded for doing so. But their drawings were of lower quality when they were "working" for someone else. Their interest in drawing was reduced by the experience. When they had a chance to draw during free playtime a week or two later, they chose it much less often than the children who had not been rewarded for their artwork.

These findings suggest that when we are first introducing an activity such as drawing to children, or hoping to encourage a greater interest in it by those who have avoided it, offering some kind of reward can help. But when we are working with children who already have their own interest in drawing (or any other form of expression, in all likelihood), offering them a reward can backfire. An external reward can undercut their interest in doing the activity on their own.

This unusual finding is explained by the over-justification hypothesis. When children already have their own reason for drawing (because they enjoy it), but we give them the added reason of doing it for an external reward, they may come to think they are doing it just for the reward. The quality of their work drops, and when we stop offering the reward, they stop doing it. By "over-justifying" the activity, we have undercut the child's intrinsic motivation. *Intrinsic motivation* is the child's own desire to do things. *Extrinsic motivation* is the desire to do something because of an external reward or punishment. Early care and education programs hope that children's intrinsic motivation—to draw, to read, to learn, to try hard, to do good work—will increase over time. We don't want children to do well only when they expect a reward. We want them to do their best and to enjoy their work on their own, to become self-directing and self-motivating. The study above shows that extrinsic rewards (a gold star, a certificate, our praise) can help a child learn to enjoy an activity such as drawing at first, but then later we should pull back from too many external rewards, allow the children to do the activity because they love it, and possibly help the children recognize that they love doing the activity for themselves.

 *Practice Tip*

Working with Preschoolers

- Provide children with examples of fine art. Post prints from famous artists around the classroom, a still life of fruit by the eating area, portraits of people and families in the dramatic play area, and paintings of houses and buildings in the block area. Change the art regularly. Sources for artwork might include inexpensive prints found in craft stores, on the Internet, or in books, or prints borrowed from the local library.

- Take field trips to art museums and art studios. Invite local artists to come and explain how they create their art or even give a simple art lesson to the children.

- Provide a variety of art materials accessible to the children throughout the day. Go beyond markers, crayons, and playdough to offer pastels, colored chalk, real clay, watercolors, and more, changing the materials regularly. Find a wide variety of paints, drawing tools, and other materials to use as art media.

- Provide different sizes and types of brushes and other tools for painting. Sponges, eyedroppers, or even turkey basters can be used with paint. Kitchen implements of all types can be interesting art tools. (Ever make a print with a potato masher?)

- Provide other tools for making prints: cut sponge shapes (purchased and homemade), apple halves (find the star shape inside), or celery stalk bottoms (makes a beautiful rose shape). Send parents and children on a hunt to find new tools for printing.

- Provide a variety of surfaces to paint or draw on, not just white or colored construction paper. Use newsprint, tag board, grocery bags, butcher paper, wrapping paper, tissue paper, cardboard boxes, and scrap mail.

- Provide other materials to be combined with art materials for experimenting. Add craft sticks and gummed colored paper or precut shapes and straws to make collages. Provide magazines and scissors for cutting, and save scrap paper for cutting to make interesting collages. Stencils provide some assistance in creating shapes and objects but can be limiting in many ways, so don't overuse them. Texture boards for crayon rubbing make it easy for younger children to explore new results on their paper, but it is better to collect real items (like leaves) for making rubbings.

- Provide materials and tools for children to create sculptures and other three-dimensional art, such as craft dough, clay, wood, wire, and straws.

- Art materials should be accessible to children throughout the day, during "art time," and as a choice during free play.

- Talk to children about the actions they are using and the results on the paper. Comment on details of their drawings or the connections to their recent experiences. "You made lots of small lines on this part of your picture, but over here, it has big blotches of blue and green." "Look at how you combined the red and yellow here on your drawing to make orange." "This brown figure reminds me of the dog we saw on our walk today."

- Support children in their use of art materials to help them represent and understand events and experiences. "We are taking the crayons and paper outside today so you can draw something that you see out in the play yard." Ask children to make a picture after a field trip of something they remember. Talk about the experience as they are drawing. Ask them to describe what they remember and to add details to their description as they draw.

- Help children recognize and explore basic art principles. These main principles are often described as the different dimensions of art: line, shape, form, color, texture, and space. Help children explore different kinds of:

  - *lines:* straight, curved, wiggly, thin, fat, jagged

  - *shapes:* regular shapes such as circles, squares, or triangles, and irregular shapes like blobs

  - *form:* having a three-dimensional form—using clay, wood, or other construction materials

  - *color:* naming specific colors, but also classifying them as warm or cool colors, light or dark, bright or dull

  - *texture:* add texture to paint with sand or coffee grounds, use puffy paint, different collage materials such as fabric, sandpaper, bark, or netting

> ◆ *space:* positive space (space taken up by objects)
> or negative space (space that is between objects)
>
> Describe these principles and elements as you talk with children about their art.

Encouraging Children's Aesthetic Responses to Art

After studying how children and adults come to understand art, one scientist has proposed that there are five stages in aesthetic development: (1) favoritism, (2) beauty and realism, (3) expressiveness, (4) style and form, and (5) autonomy (Parsons 1987). One research study examined whether preschool children's responses to art could be understood according to these stages. Three- to five-year-olds were involved in a special four-week program during the summer at their early care and education program that emphasized the visual arts. Teachers led many conversations with students about different famous paintings, such as those by Leonardo da Vinci, Mary Cassatt, and Jackson Pollock.

They found that at the beginning of the program, children's responses corresponded to stage one of the theory, called favoritism. During this stage, children are learning to understand what a painting is and what it can represent. They respond mainly to the colors used in the artwork. Children also prefer paintings depicting familiar things, places, or events. For example, when teachers asked children why they did or did not like a particular painting, one child responded that she liked a painting "because it has all the water and it kind of reminds me of my vacations" (Schiller 1995).

After many conversations about paintings, children began to respond according to stage two of the theory, called beauty and realism. At this stage, children become more focused on the subject matter and are concerned with how "true to life" the painting is. Children like paintings when they look realistic. For example, after showing a Picasso painting, the teacher asked the children, "What do you think of that? Are the colors bright or what?" One child responded, "It doesn't look real." Other children agreed that they would rather the painting look real.

Children tend to move into the later stages in this theory, of expressiveness, style and form, and artistic autonomy, at later ages. But this research shows that even young children are capable of talking about and responding to art. When given the opportunity, they can begin to proceed through the early stages of aesthetic development.

Promoting Preschoolers' Appreciation for All Art Styles

Children generally like things that are familiar. Just like familiar toys, books, music, or food, the artwork we place in children's daily surroundings will influence their artistic preferences.

This idea was demonstrated by a study in which preschoolers (from three to five years old) were asked to choose their favorite paintings. Researchers found that children generally prefer abstract art (art that attempts to convey feelings and ideas rather than images) and realistic art (art of images as true to life as possible) rather than stylistic art (art that distorts images to emphasize style and form) (Bowker and Sawyers 1988).

After learning this, the researchers exposed the children to a stylistic painting (one of the least favorite paintings among the children) in three different ways. Some children saw the painting on the wall of their early care and education classroom for six weeks. Others saw the painting on their bedroom wall at home for six weeks. Finally, some children participated in discussions of the painting and artist with an art teacher in their early care and education program.

Researchers found that the children's preferences for stylistic paintings in general (not just this one painting) increased after being exposed to a stylistic painting in any one of the three ways. Many children who had the painting in their bedroom said that the stylistic painting was their favorite because they owned it. The children in the other two groups often said that they liked the painting because they recognized it from their classroom.

Art as a Process of Play, and Art as a Product

Is art a verb (something we do) or a noun (an object we create)? It is, of course, both. First, it is a form of creative expression. The act of creation is fun, and art is a form of play for both children and adults. This view of art is often called "art as a process," meaning that the process of doing art is an important thing, much more important than the end product.

Some forms of art have a product that we care about. When scribbles start turning into letters, we point out the ones that are especially well formed and give them a name. "Look, here is an 'E' just like in your name!" When the representational drawing of an older preschooler becomes recognizable as a house, we (and the child) are so impressed that we show it to the parent at the end of the day.

In the current atmosphere of standards and accountability, some parents have become more interested in their children's achievements in art (their products), rather than the children's enjoyment of making art (the process). They may push their children, and their children's teachers, to make drawings that are more realistic in representing objects or events. Teachers need to respect the wishes of parents but also should inform them about the value of experimentation and play in art.

MISTAKEN PRACTICE

Turning Art Play into Work

What We Saw

Provide precut parts and directions for creating a specific art project. For example, after a trip to the farm, provide pink circles for children to make a pig, or precut orange circles and black triangles to make pumpkins.

Why It Doesn't Work

Art projects like this are mostly an exercise in following directions. This is more like learning to solve a puzzle, where there is only one correct answer, than doing art, where there are an unlimited number of solutions. Learning to follow the teacher's directions, and to carefully produce the same finished product as everyone else, is a useful skill, but it is not art. In the above example, much of the work is done by the teacher, not the child (deciding what will be made and cutting out the shapes). There is little opportunity for children to represent what they have experienced, express their feelings or ideas, or create something unique or imaginative. Even when teachers accept any placement of the parts and the resulting product, children recognize whether or not their product is "right."

Why We See This Mistaken Practice

Most adults had this kind of art activity when they were children and might not know a different way to present art experiences. Also, teachers feel pressure to send children home with these products as evidence to parents that children are productive during the day.

What Would Work Better

Talk about the experiences and ideas children have. You might even show them pictures of pigs and pumpkins while you are talking about their firsthand experiences. Then provide open-ended art materials for the children to use in representing their experiences in unique ways. Provide parents with information on the value of art exploration, and provide photos and observation notes of children's activities during the day, as evidence of children's rich learning through play.

Programs with a successful *process approach* to art have conscious policies, teacher training, and parent education components. Often orientation manuals for teachers include sections on promoting process art. Classrooms include open art centers offering many opportunities for children to explore the process of creation with a variety of materials. Signs are posted by the parent area or children's art displays, educating parents about the value of process art, and parent handbooks explain the benefits of process art.

When children make paintings or play in the sandbox, are they using their intelligence, are they making art, or are they playing? It would seem that all these descriptions could be true. At these moments, the recognition and reinforcement that teachers provide to young children about their creativity and artistic ability can lay a foundation for a creative life. When a teacher says, "Tell me about what you are making," this helps the child feel valued as a creative individual. It also asks the child to conceptualize her experience with words, which leads to greater understanding. Leading theorists of child development, such as Piaget (1951) and Vygotsky (1978), have noted that the development of symbols and symbolic capacities, which often takes place in children's play, is an essential foundation for language, concept formation, and other aspects of intellectual functioning (a topic we address in chapter 5). When we make art into a playful process, rather than an exercise in copying someone else's model of a product, we open much greater potential to stimulate the intellectual growth of young children.

The Reggio Emilia Approach: Emphasizing Fine Arts in Preschool Settings

Good early childhood programs include daily art activities that are child-centered and highlight the process rather than the product of the children's creations. Art easels, drawing paper, collage materials, and other art materials are available for children daily. But in Reggio Emilia programs, the arts are not one of many activities; they are the heart of the program. The entire classroom becomes an extension of the child's creative efforts, and all aspects of intellectual and social development take place in the context of children's art activities.

Put very simply, the Reggio approach believes that very young children can become engrossed in long-term, creative projects if properly stimulated, nurtured, and guided (Edwards, Gandini, and Forman 1998). The foundation of the program is fine arts, with special attention paid to creating works of art, writing about experiences, and directing conversation. When properly implemented, Reggio programs aim to allow children to speak in all their languages, "expressive, communicative, symbolic, cognitive, ethical, metaphorical, logical, imaginative, and relational" (Municipality of Reggio Emilia 1997: 19).

The Municipality of Reggio Emilia, in Italy, began developing its preschool program in 1963 and added an infant-toddler component in 1970. Since then, thousands of early childhood educators from many countries have visited the city to see for themselves what is so special about this approach. What becomes immediately apparent is that Reggio classrooms do not look like classic North American early childhood classrooms. Missing are the plastic furnishings in primary colors, the cute posters, and the bordered bulletin boards. Instead, a table might be set with a cut-glass vase filled with fresh flowers on top of a lace tablecloth. The classrooms abound in natural colors and natural lighting and look more like an extension of home than a classroom. Each classroom or set of classrooms have access to an *atelier* or a *mini-atelier*. An *atelier* is an "art studio, a place devoted to the development of visual and graphic arts" (Rabitti 2007: 1). The atelier is the focal area for children to become masterful in all kinds of experiential art, including drawing, painting, and working with clay. It also serves as a lab where adults can learn how children master concepts and solve problems. The teacher who staffs the atelier is called an *atelierista*, and she designs the studio to meet the needs of the children. The atelierista is in close contact with the other classroom teachers and meets with them to preplan the projects.

Reggio Example: Creating the Bird Playground

In one of the famous projects that brought the Reggio approach to worldwide attention, preschoolers in LaVilletta school in Italy designed an amusement park for birds (Forman 2007). Observant teachers noted that the children enjoyed the birds that visited the bird feeders each day and brought that observation to a planning session that included the atelierista. Cooperatively, the teaching staff came up with ideas and materials that might pique the children's interest. Children were given opportunities to study water wheels and created wind-powered wheels to be certain the birds had water. They made swings of varying sizes to accommodate different birds. They studied the birds and the kinds of food they eat. The teachers provided the children with the materials they needed, including books about birds and construction. They encouraged the children to make blueprints to be certain the structures they created could fit the allowable space outside. The project lasted for weeks, and the end result was a fabulous bird amusement park. All the staff, children, and their families celebrated its opening day.

One key to this type of approach is very careful planning that involves all the staff. The atelierista, in cooperation with other teachers, designs the lesson plans around the project. All projects are based on observations made about things that interest the children. The children could not complete the projects without directed conversation by the teachers who ask questions that challenge the children to think and problem solve. In addition, the supplies must be ample enough so the children can see their plans become real.

BRINGING REGGIO PRACTICES TO OTHER CLASSROOMS

To implement a true Reggio approach is difficult without really studying it, visiting Reggio schools, and attending Reggio conferences. However, there are parts of the approach that can be used to enhance any early childhood art program.

1. Give children a chance to plan what they want to draw, paint, or create. Ask questions about what materials they might need or what research they might need to do before starting the project. If a child wants to draw a flower, you could bring in books with pictures of flowers, bring in real flowers, and help the children mix colors to achieve the desired look.

2. Document the children's progress. Do not let the thought of documentation translate into a lot more work. Keep note cards in your pockets and jot down what the children say they are creating. If the child is making a two-dimensional picture, you can write on the surface or the back of the paper what the child says he has created. Later, you can help the child recall the work or call it to the attention of his parents. If it is three-dimensional, challenge the child to give the work a title.

3. Let children work on an art project for more than a day, or until they become bored. Be an active observer to be able to add to the children's work. If they are drawing flowers, will the activity extend to a study of creating fragrances, or shadows, or vases?

4. Give children a variety of mediums, and display them in an inviting, attractive manner. Reggio classrooms keep supplies in open bins, sometimes with glass sides, that may be color coordinated. Red crayons, paint, paper, and yarn might be sorted together and blend into the oranges, yellows, and other colors.

5. Display children's artwork as if it is priceless. Children value what adults value. If the work is matted or set apart on a table or shelf, children know their efforts are respected.

6. When possible, discuss art projects with other teachers. This helps not only in your own planning, but also will give you ideas to expand the projects. Remember that the bird amusement park idea came from an observant teacher sharing her ideas with her colleagues.

Reggio Teachers

Not only the environment and art studios set Reggio schools apart from their counterparts. Reggio schools also enthusiastically embrace the infusion of liberal arts into the professional discipline of early childhood education. Teachers at these schools are not necessarily artists (although some truly are). They do believe, however, that through cooperation, research, and continuous documentation of children's progress they can encourage creativity and create environments that foster curiosity about the beautiful world and unique culture that is inherent in each child. Teachers do not shy away from any topic that might be of interest to a child. The "100 Languages of Children Art Exhibit," which has toured the world, showcases pieces completed by children in the Italian Reggio schools, including art projects addressing pregnancy and birth, seeds becoming oak trees, and visual representations of the water wheels that make up part of the bird amusement park (Municipality of Reggio Emilia 1997). The teachers believe that children can learn to dissect complex problems with the proper encouragement and questioning by trained adult observers.

Reggio teachers also encourage children to represent their ideas in different ways. They ask questions that encourage children to organize their thoughts. They challenge children to draw what they want to create. They may offer children the chance to represent the same idea three-dimensionally with different materials. Teachers understand that sometimes children demonstrate their ideas better on paper than in words. The whole approach centers on appreciation of the child as the creator.

Reggio teachers refer to themselves as researchers of early childhood, and as a result, they document children's progress on the projects they design. Project notes are often hung in binders near where the children are working. In this way, any teacher may add to the notes, and any observer may read a daily account of progress. Children's comments are copied verbatim and added to the notes. The projects can shift and change direction depending on the children's ideas, which are often illuminated by the skilled questions teachers ask to get clarification about what the children are thinking. Often teachers take pictures of the progress, step by step, so that children can reflect on the steps involved in completion. Sometimes, after completion of an extended project, project notes are put into a book format along with pictures. This provides an opportunity for children to share with parents and one another as they move to a new plan. Children's input is highly respected, and the work in progress is protected so that it can be left at day's end in its various stages of completion.

Reggio Art Materials

Art materials that are used in Reggio schools are also different from what might be seen in other preschools. Unlike many preschools, there is no playdough in Reggio classrooms. Instead, clay is the favored medium for three-dimensional projects, and some ateliers are equipped with kilns. At first look, it seems dull to see the children working with plain gray or brown clay, and it is certainly harder to manipulate after using the soft consistency of artificial molding materials. However, the Reggio approach stresses the natural, and children are taught to patiently knead the clay with water until it can be molded. Children are kept in small groups, and the atelierista sits in their midst, questioning them and documenting their work. Once completed, the creations are allowed to harden, and if the center has a kiln, they are fired.

Another difference in this approach is that Reggio teachers are comfortable with being provocateurs. They support and stimulate learning, which includes challenging children to think. They seek to understand what the children value in their work and then find ways to emphasize that value, rather than worrying about getting something done on time or cleaning up in a timely manner. When implemented in its purest form, the Reggio approach is stimulating and beautiful to witness. The Reggio approach uses art as the medium for all the learning of the early care and education program.

Conclusion

Beginning in infancy, children are developing artistic skills. After experimenting with making marks on paper and using a variety of art mediums, children gradually learn that they can represent the world around them in their artwork. Learning to draw also supports children's growing literacy skills. Teachers-caregivers can promote this developing process by noticing children's interests and providing materials and feedback to support them. They can also introduce children to a wide variety of artists and artwork to help develop children's interest and appreciation for art.

Further Reading

On Research

Baghban, M. 2007. Scribbles, labels, and stories: The role of drawing in the development of writing. *Young Children* 62 (1): 20–26.

Golomb, C. 2004. *The child's creation of a pictorial world*. 2nd ed. Mahwah, NJ: Erlbaum.

Herberloz, B., and L. Hanson. 1995. *Early childhood art*. 5th ed. Madison, WI: Brown and Benchmark Publishers.

Schiller, M. 1995. Reggio Emilia: A focus on emergent curriculum and art. *Art Education* 3:45–50.

On Practice

Baghban, M. 2007. Scribbles, labels, and stories: The role of drawing in the development of writing. *Young Children* 62 (1): 20–26.

Colbert, C. 1997. Visual arts in the developmentally appropriate integrated curriculum. In *Integrated curriculum and developmentally appropriate practice: Birth to age eight*, eds. C. H. Hart and D. C. Burst. Albany, NY: State University of New York Press.

Epstein, A. S. 2001. Thinking about art: Encouraging art appreciation in early childhood settings. *Young Children* 56 (3): 38–43.

Feeney, S., and E. Moravchik. 1987. A thing of beauty: Aesthetic development in young children. *Young Children* 42 (6): 7–15.

Jalongo, M. R. 1999. How we respond to the artistry of children: Ten barriers to overcome. *Early Childhood Education Journal* 26 (4): 205–208.

Mitchell, S. T., M. H. Johnson, and R. Althouse. 2003. *The colors of learning: Integrating the visual arts into the early childhood curriculum*. Washington, D.C.: National Association for the Education of Young Children and Teachers College Press.

Pelo, A. 2007. *The Language of art: Inquiry-based studio practices in early childhood settings*. Saint Paul, MN: Redleaf Press.

Thompson, S. C. 2005. *Children as illustrators: Making meaning through art and language*. Washington, D.C.: National Association for the Education of Young Children.

Zimmerman, E., and L. Zimmerman. 2000. Art education and early childhood education: The young child as creator and meaning maker within a community contest. *Young Children* 55 (6): 87–92.

Children's Books

Browne, A. 2000. *Willy's pictures.* Cambridge, MA: Candlewick Press.

Canning, K. 1979. *A painted tale.* New York: Barron's.

Carle, E. 1992. *Draw me a star.* New York: Philomel Books.

Clayton, E. 1996. *Ella's trip to the museum.* New York: Crown Publishers.

Demi. 1980. *Liang and the magic paintbrush.* New York: Henry Holt.

dePaola, T. 1989. *The art lesson.* New York: Putnam.

Ehlert, L. *Red leaf, yellow leaf.* 1991. San Diego: Harcourt Brace Jovanovich.

Hoban, T. 1989. *Of colors and things.* New York: Greenwillow Books.

Hubbard, P. 1996. *My crayons talk.* New York: Henry Holt.

Johnson, C. 1955. *Harold and the purple crayon.* New York: HarperCollins.

Lionni, L. 1959. *Little blue and little yellow.* New York: Mulberry Books.

Metropolitan Museum of Art. 2005. *Museum shapes.* New York: Little, Brown and Co.

Moss, M. 1990. *Regina's big mistake.* Boston: Houghton Mifflin.

Micklethwait, L. 2006. *Children: A first art book.* Berkeley, CA: Publishers Group West.

Shaw, C. G. 2000. *It looked like spilt milk.* New York: HarperCollins.

Sohl, M. E. 1993. *Look what I did with a leaf!* New York: Walker.

Sortland, B. 1999. *Anna's art adventure.* Minneapolis, MN: Carolrhoda Books.

Turner, R. M. 1993. *Faith Ringgold.* Boston: Little, Brown and Co.

Walsh, E. S. 1989. *Mouse paint*. San Diego: Harcourt Brace Jovanovich.

Williams, K. L. 1998. *Painted dreams*. New York: Lothrop, Lee, and Shephard.

Ziefert, H. 2003. *Lunchtime for a purple snake*. Boston: Houghton Mifflin.

~~~~~~

When Teachers Reflect: *Staying True to Art as a Process*

As an early childhood professional, you know the value of *process art* with children and how it stimulates their creativity and developmental learning. Lately, however, parents have been complaining that their children bring home too much artwork that doesn't look like anything. There are several other teachers in your program that plan a great deal of *product art*, and parents are starting to comment to the director that some rooms have more cute art projects than others have. The director brings this up at a staff meeting, and you are asked to explain why your art projects are not more appealing to parents.

- ♦ How will you explain what children learn through the art process?

- ♦ How could you talk to parents about the value of exploration with art materials?

- ♦ How can you display the artwork to make it more aesthetically pleasing to parents?

- ♦ What research or professional reference could you use to justify your approach to art?

~~~~~~

Letter to Parents

Dear Parents,

Do you remember the first box of crayons you received as a child? Do you remember carefully using each one on a sheet of paper to see what beautiful colors you could draw? Have you gone to the beach and built a sandcastle, only to see it washed away the next time you visited the beach? Art is many things to many people. To children, art is a way to express creativity and understanding of the world. A child may see a rainbow in the sky and then want to draw it. It doesn't matter if the child got the right colors in the right order. It matters that the child is inspired enough to try.

We want to work with you to help your child develop imagination and creativity. How can we do this together?

At school, we will do the following:

- Plan creative art activities that let children explore how they see their world.

- Provide a variety of materials for children to use in their exploration.

- Display children's artwork on the walls to create a sense of pride in accomplishment.

- Value individual work in all art projects.

- Minimize the use of teacher patterns that children have to follow.

- Ask children to talk about their art experience and write what they say.

At home, you could do the following:

- Display your child's artwork on the refrigerator or in other special places. How about in her room? (Hint: put it at her eye level.)

- Ask your child to tell you about his art project. Use open-ended questions such as "Tell me about your picture." Also, describe their picture in terms such

From *Intellectual Development: Connecting Science and Practice in Early Childhood Settings* (Redleaf Press, 2009).

as color, texture, and shape. "I see you used lots of yellow paint and put big circles at the bottom."

- Tell your child that you cannot save every picture she makes. Involve your child in the process of deciding which ones to keep in a special box, which ones to discard, and which ones are so special that your child wants to keep them on the wall for a long time.

- Enjoy the process of art yourself with your child. Make playdough, paint with watercolors, and sculpt with sand. (If you would like recipes for playdough, clay, or paint, please let us know. We would be happy to share.)

Did You Know?

Children who are better at drawing also tend to have larger vocabularies and better preliteracy skills. Art is a way to communicate (visually) and is linked to these other ways to communicate (through the spoken and written word).

Having fun with art experiences can build the foundation for increased competence in many parts of your child's life.

From *Intellectual Development: Connecting Science and Practice in Early Childhood Settings* (Redleaf Press, 2009).

5

Why We Don't Give Away the Right Answer

Cognitive Development

When Juan's mother dropped him off forty-five minutes early, his teacher, Dave, had to find something to keep Juan occupied while the teachers prepared the classroom for the day. The teacher looked at Juan, then looked at the rack of puzzles, ranging from simple twelve-piece sets to much more complex fifty-piece sets. He picked one, gave it to Juan, and went back to mixing playdough. Juan went to work and struggled with the puzzle for about twenty-five minutes, almost quitting once (Dave gave him a hint at that point), but finally completed this particular puzzle for the first time ever, with considerable pride.

When asked why he picked that particular puzzle, Dave explained that if the puzzle was too easy, Juan would finish it too quickly and get bored. If it was too hard, Juan would give up. To capture Juan's attention for the longest possible time, the teacher had compared the complexity of Juan's current thinking abilities with the complexity of the various puzzles. He selected a puzzle that was just slightly more complex than Juan's current ability, but close enough so Juan could sense that he might be able to figure it out. This level of challenge would be the most highly motivating to Juan, and if he succeeded in solving the puzzle, then his own thinking would have grown in complexity through mastering the challenge.

Early Cognitive Development Matters

When young children develop their abilities in one area, they often do better in other areas as well. For example, increasing musical skills somehow causes improved math performance (chapter 3), and drawing ability is somehow related to vocabulary size (chapter 4). These are surprising findings, leading us to ask: why are these very different skills related?

To answer that question, this chapter considers the child's overall cognitive development. When children learn math or music, they are learning the content of each subject, but at the same time they are also increasing the complexity of their thinking in general. We call this general thinking ability *cognitive development*. It is based upon the amazing growth of the child's brain in the first three years of life, in particular the proliferation of neurons (the building blocks of the brain), as well as the pathways (dendrites) and connections between the neurons (synapses). The degree to which neural pathways are activated (through early experience) and connected with each other determines the child's potential to learn. Scientists have discovered that the rate of brain growth during the first few years of life is very unequal among children, in large part because of differences in children's early experiences. This causes huge differences in children's current and future ability to learn and to succeed. No other period of intellectual development is as important for success across the whole life span than the first few years of life. Therefore, it is no exaggeration to claim that teachers in early care and education programs are the most important teachers in children's lives.

Recent research demonstrates that brain growth and cognitive development are directly affected by the child's environments and experiences (Kuhl 1994). Newborns are born with over a hundred billion neurons in their brains, and by the time they reach fifteen months old, each neuron will have grown over fifteen hundred dendrites (connections) with other neurons (Thompson 2000). The toddler brain is twice as dense as an adult brain and twice as active (Bergen & Coscia 2000). The environment in which infants and toddlers spend their first few years determines which of these neural pathways are activated and which are selectively pruned through lack of use. Because of the effect of early experience upon the growth and structuring of the brain, some children will take powerful mental computers (brains) into their adolescence and adulthood, while others will not. The activation and strengthening of neural pathways is the physical change in the brain that creates cognitive development in the child. Because this development is a physical change in the brain, early cognitive development has lifelong consequences for attachment, perception, learning, social interaction, self-regulation, and language development. Every thought and every feeling begins in the neural structures of the brain. Not surprisingly, children who develop their cognitive (or thinking) abilities at a younger age tend to do better in their later schooling and social lives. Thus, early cognitive development significantly influences the child's future life path (Nelson, Thomas, and De Haan 2006; Schweinhart et al. 2005).

Three long-term studies of model programs of early care and education have demonstrated the lifelong benefits of early cognitive stimulation.

✔ *Practice Tip*

Supporting Cognitive Development

Provide a Safe Environment

- Eliminate potential hazards both indoors and out (cover electrical outlets, fence outdoor play areas, put cushions under climbing equipment, avoid clutter).
- Provide "defensible spaces" for children to play in alone with a toy and "cozy spaces" for two children to play in together and to feel safe from intrusion.
- Provide adequate supervision at all times.

Provide for Security (a necessary prerequisite to exploration)

- Schedule consistent caregivers (attachment groupings, regular staff assignment, low staff turnover).
- Maintain consistent routines (predictable daily activities schedule, care routines that coordinate with family practices, adults who describe what will happen next).
- Provide a sense of belonging with individual cubbies or family photos.
- Meet children's needs promptly, appropriately, and sensitively.

The High/Scope Perry Preschool Project in Ypsilanti, Michigan (Schwein-hart et al. 2005), the Abecedarian Project in North Carolina (Campbell et al. 2001), and the Child-Parent Centers in Chicago (Reynolds, Temple, Robertson, and Mann 2001) were experiments in which some children received the model program while similar children did not. The children were followed into adolescence and adulthood to see if the program caused differences in children's life outcomes.

Figure 5.1

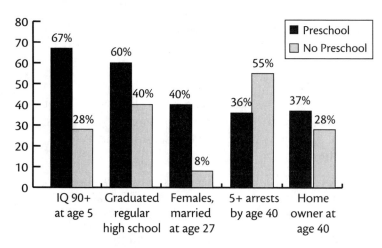

Benefits of the Perry Preschool Program up to Age 40 (Schweinhart et al. 2005)

These three programs differed from most early care and education programs in at least two important ways. First, the teachers in these model programs received specialized training in stimulating the mental development of children. The programs used specific curricula (learning activities) that were designed to reflect our best understandings about children's cognitive development. Second, the programs included very strong parent education components. Although the three model programs had somewhat different approaches, the researchers who investigated each one reached the same conclusion: early care and education programs can have dramatic, long-term benefits, and the benefits become more pronounced with time, as the children progress through school and into adulthood.

Figure 5.1 shows some of the results for the children who attended the Perry Preschool as compared to equivalent children from the same neighborhoods who did not. Summarizing the results up to age forty, we can see the following about the Perry Preschool children:

- They experienced an immediate improvement in IQ scores.
- They completed high school far more often.
- They avoided crime far more than their peers did.
- The girls were five times more likely to be married during their prime child-bearing years.
- They were much more likely to own a home at age forty (and also to have a job and a savings account).

Figure 5.2

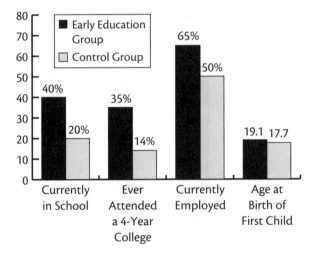

Benefits of the Carolina Abecedarian Project at Age 21
(Campbell et al. 2001)

The results for the Abecedarian program were very similar, as shown in Figure 5.2. By age twenty-one, the children who attended the model program:

- succeeded more in their educations, even attending college;
- were more likely to be employed;
- were delaying childbearing by about one-and-a-half years, getting themselves out of school and into jobs before starting their families.

The results for the Chicago Child-Parent Centers program in Figure 5.3 are consistent with the first two studies. The children who received the model program:

- had significantly higher math and reading scores during their school years;

- were almost half as likely to have been retained in grade;

- by age twenty, were far more likely to have finished high school and to have avoided arrest. (In other words, the same story of life-changing impacts.)

The outcomes from these three studies demonstrate that when we provide children, in the earliest years of life, with experiences and environments aimed at stimulating their cognitive development, they not only perform better on later cognitive tasks (such as IQ tests and school success) but also on the tasks of successful adult living.

Figure 5.3

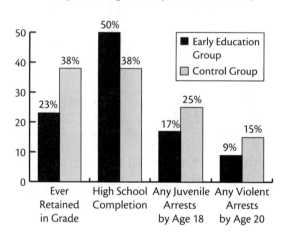

Benefits of the Chicago Child-Parent Center Program at Age 20 (Reynolds et al. 2001)

What Kinds of Early Experiences Make the Difference for Cognitive Development?

What should teachers (and parents) do, or avoid doing, if they wish to promote young children's brain growth and cognitive development? We answer this question in several ways. First, we describe the findings of research on children who receive too little or too much sensory stimulation in early childhood. Then we summarize three prominent theories that are useful in understanding how children's thinking abilities grow. Last, we summarize the research that has looked carefully at the children who are the most intelligent in early childhood to see what their parents and teachers are doing that encourages their superior cognitive development.

The Effects of Too Little Sensory Stimulation on Cognitive Development

To develop their thinking capacities, young children need experiences, which come to the child through the senses. Sensory input such as touch, smell, sound, taste, and conversation with others are essential components of the average expectable environment for young children. For example, we saw in chapter 1 that the amount of language interaction experienced by young children has a predictable effect on how quickly their vocabularies grow. But what about the effect of low sensory stimulation on the child's cognitive development or ability to learn?

Researchers have given us a poignant example of how sensory deprivation can lead to the lack of mental and social development. A girl named Genie was kept in an attic room by her parents, chained to her potty chair during the day and in her crib at night (Rymer 1994). She received minimal care: diapered, bathed, and fed. Her parents did not speak with her, and she had no other human contact. When discovered by a social worker at age thirteen, Genie had poor social skills and no language skills. Two married researchers eventually brought Genie into their home to help her develop language and social skills. To their surprise, after two years of intense training, Genie was still unable to learn any meaningful language or social skills. Her lack of cognitive development during the crucial early years when her brain was creating its basic structures made the learning of language as a thirteen-year-old almost impossible (Rymer 1994).

This example illustrates the effects of impeded cognitive development on language and social development, and researchers believe the same idea applies across all areas of learning. The early childhood years are a crucial period for humans to receive a wide variety of experiences. Depriving children of varied sensory stimulation in the early years places them at a significant disadvantage in life. They can continue to learn and change at any later age, but doing so is much more difficult than if they had the advantage of a stimulating early childhood.

The Effects of Too Much Sensory Stimulation on Cognitive Development

Can a child receive too much stimulation? This may come as a surprise, but the answer is yes. Some adults are intrusive, insisting on the child's

✓ *Practice Tip*

Supporting Cognitive Development

Provide a Rich, Aesthetically Pleasing Environment

- Provide natural as well as artificial lighting.
- Use neutral colors for the walls and furnishings, so play materials stand out rather than get lost in "visual noise."
- Give the eye places to rest (this is essential for moving information from short-term to long-term memory).
- Organize spaces well, with a clear arrangement of areas.
  - Eliminate clutter, which can cause behavioral problems.
  - Create enough space for children to move freely without crowding.
- Provide a balanced variety of objects for sensory exploration and different types of play.
- Use open-ended materials for exploration and experimentation.
- Provide a variety of props and clothing for dramatic play on different themes.
- Frequently rotate materials, balancing the familiar with the new.

Plan for and Support Child-Directed Learning

- Allow time for uninterrupted play.
- Encourage hands-on exploration.
- Observe children's play to appreciate the learning involved.
- Provide attention and support for children's discoveries.

- ◆ Wait for children to attempt to solve their own problems.

- ◆ When helping, provide the minimum amount of help needed to solve the problem.

- ◆ Encourage children to interact with and learn from one another.

attention even when the child is ready to rest. Fortunately, even infants have ways of tuning out most overstimulation by well-meaning adults. They simply turn away from a too-insistent adult playing peekaboo, thus lowering their level of arousal (Brazelton, Koslowski, and Main 1974).

However, there is a group of children for whom overstimulation is common, beyond their control, and over time, actually becomes necessary for their continued survival: maltreated young children. Due to their experiences, maltreated children become hypervigilant to impending maltreatment. At the earliest sign that an adult might mistreat them, these children's brains are flushed with the hormone cortisol, greatly increasing their arousal. Cortisol is the hormone that gives us the "fight or flight" response when we are frightened. High levels of cortisol can destroy neurons, thereby reducing the number of synapses (connections) in the brain. Besides destroying brain cells, this state of constant alertness affects brain growth in a second, possibly more important way. Experience sculpts the brain of maltreated children so that they come to perceive the world differently than other children. The neural pathways of maltreated children become fine-tuned to notice any hint of danger (Pollack and Sinha 2002). Because the brains of these children spend so much energy growing the neural pathways necessary for avoiding maltreatment, they spend less effort on creating the brain structures for normal cognitive development. This helps explain why they do less well on cognitive tests and school performance (Kurtz et al. 1993; Vondra, Barnett, and Cicchetti 1990).

Most children feel safe and free to explore their world, creating new neural pathways that represent new things they have learned. But maltreated children explore less because their brains are occupied looking for signs of trouble. They miss the opportunities to discover new things and, thus, the opportunity to develop new neural pathways that add to their knowledge of the world.

✅ *Practice Tip*

Supporting Cognitive Development

Promote Learning by Adding Words or Labels to Children's Play

- sensory experiences ("The duck is soft and fluffy.")
- objects ("You can see the bird at the window!")
- concepts ("Your diaper is wet." "The ball is round.")
- actions ("You pushed the ball . . .")
- effects (". . . and the ball rolled away.")
- relationships between things ("The round shape fits into the round hole.")
- feelings ("You're sad because mom had to leave." "You really want that toy, but can't reach it.")
- questions ("What will happen if we add water to the dirt?")

Read Books with Children

- Select books that match the child's developmental level and interests.
- Make group reading time interactive and fun.
- Provide lap time for looking at books one-on-one where you do the following:
  - Talk about the pictures.
  - Point to and name objects and characters.
  - Describe actions.
  - Predict what will happen next.
  - Ask open-ended questions to engage higher-level thinking ("What do you think will happen if Pooh sticks his head in the hole?" "Why do you think Max said that to his mom?").

Neglected children receive far too little sensory input, while abused children receive way too much. In both cases, the brain is affected in ways that drastically reduce the child's cognitive development, now and in the future. In between these extremes, most children receive experiences that are at the right level of sensory stimulation, but which can still vary widely in their effects on cognitive development. This leads to a big question: how does experience lead to growth in intelligence, and what kinds of experiences are best at promoting cognitive development? To answer these questions, we next describe three theories on how children's thinking develops: Piaget's Theory of Cognitive Development, Vygotsky's Theory of Socio-Cultural Development, and Information Processing Theory.

Piaget's Theory of Cognitive Development

Jean Piaget was a Swiss-born psychologist who was among the first to believe that children did not think like adults. Before Piaget, scientists and educators believed that children simply knew less than adults, but Piaget demonstrated that children are also different from adults in how they think about what they know. This insight was made by Piaget in the 1920s when he noticed that children's incorrect answers to intelligence tests were not random, but wrong in systematic, patterned ways, which showed their logic was different from adults'. This was the beginning of the study of cognitive development, and it led to Piaget's research for the next several decades. Piaget wrote in French, and his important works began to appear in English translation in the 1950s (Piaget 1950; Piaget 1952; Piaget 1954; Piaget and Inhelder 1964).

What Pushes Cognitive Development Forward?

How does a child's intelligence grow? Piaget believed that maturation (physical growth) is not enough to cause mental growth. Children also need experience with the environment. Specifically, he believed that cognitive development was an adaptive response to the environment. Adaptation is a key idea. For example, when a child feels uncomfortably cold, the body adapts by making more heat. Similarly, when a child feels discomfort because his current way of thinking cannot explain a new experience, then the child must adapt his thinking. That adaptation is cognitive development, the increasing complexity and accuracy of a child's understandings.

How does the child's thinking become more complex and more able to mentally represent the real world? Piaget believed that knowledge was held in mental ideas or concepts he called *schemas*. A useful metaphor for schemas is to think of them as files in which we store knowledge and information. When children (and adults) encounter an experience with which they have some familiarity, they add it to an existing file. When children encounter new information that cannot be assimilated into an existing file, they create a new schema: a new file in which to store the information. Therefore, "getting smarter" is an ongoing process of filling existing files with more information, creating new files with new information, and at times reorganizing the files to more correctly represent the world.

STIMULATING COGNITIVE DEVELOPMENT WITH TOYS

The human ability to play is one reason that humans develop far greater intelligence than other animals. Through play, we invent new understandings and practice new skills. This is true even for adults, but is far easier to see in young children's play. What kind of materials and toys might be best for stimulating cognitive growth? Here are three ideas.

Provide toys that can do many things, not just one thing.

Some toys only do one thing. For example, once a child can easily solve a puzzle and has done so dozens of times, the puzzle stops being so much fun. As we saw in the story of Juan at the start of this chapter, puzzles can be great for learning, but you will always need a new one that is slightly more complex than the last one.

In contrast, when toys have many uses, children will continually find new challenges in using the toy. For example, as a child becomes better at painting, the child can make more and more complex paintings with the same materials. We could say the materials adapt to the child's ability level. Other toys that can be used at many different skill levels are balls, clay, or cardboard boxes.

Use toys that put power and imagination in the child, rather than in the toy maker.

The battery-powered robot with flashing lights requires a lot of imagination by the toy maker, but the child cannot do many things with it. The robot attracts the child's immediate attention, but the child does not learn much from it and can become bored quickly.

In contrast, imagine all the things a child might do with a stuffed animal, a doll, or a toy car. These toys are simpler and can be used flexibly in many different ways. They encourage the child's imagination.

Provide toys that encourage joint activities and cooperation.

Children learn most in the company of others, in particular with mentors. A mentor can be another child with slightly greater ability. Think of materials that create joint activities. The classic examples are a ball or flying disk, items that require two to play.

Everyone has heard the old saying "Seeing is believing," but Piaget's theory of schemas turns this around into "Believing is seeing." Piaget was able to show that unless children have the schema for something (unless they have the idea of it already in their mind), they really can't see it the way an adult does. For example, Piaget showed children a set of ten sticks ordered from shortest to longest. A week later, when he asked them to draw the set of sticks, young children would draw sticks of just two lengths: a bunch of short ones next to a bunch of long ones. Six months later he asked them to recall the sticks and draw them again, and the children who had developed an understanding of seriation (the ability to order things from least to most) drew sticks reflecting the full range of sizes. Now they could really see it! Until they had the schema for seriation, they didn't see the set of sticks that way (Piaget and Inhelder 1973).

Here is an example of a powerful schema with which everyone has experience: gender. Most people, when they first encounter an infant, ask "Is it a boy or a girl?" before they will even talk to the child. Curious about this, researchers conducted a study in which they dressed a baby in either pink or blue diapers. The subjects in the study had no difficulty describing the pink-diapered infant as sweet, with delicate fingers, and a rosebud mouth. Conversely, when the same baby was wearing a blue diaper, the adults described the infant as big, with strong hands and a lusty cry (Condry and Condry 1967). People tended to see what they already knew or expected to see. Our mental schemas change our perceptions.

Humans have a strong need to make sense of what they see and then store their understanding in a schema. When we succeed in making sense of something and filing our understanding in a schema, we are in what Piaget called a state of *equilibrium*. One way to reach equilibrium is to find an existing schema in which to put new information. Piaget called this *assimilation*. We can assimilate new information with knowledge we already have. This happens when a child sees a tiny Chihuahua for the first time but successfully assimilates it into the schema for dogs. The momentary state of confusion at seeing the Chihuahua turns into equilibrium when the child assimilates the sight of the dog to her existing schema for all dogs. We are comfortable in a state of equilibrium.

PROMISING PRACTICE

Elaborating on a Child's Schema

What We Saw

Erin, a fifteen-month-old toddler, plays with a doll and sets it down on a cloth. She tries to push up her own sleeves and put the cloth around the doll. By careful observation, the teacher understands what the child is trying to do. The teacher says, "Oh, you are pushing up your sleeves just like I do when I change you. Do you want to change this baby like I change you?" Erin smiles yes. The teacher helps Erin pretend to change the doll's diaper while describing with words what they are doing. ("Now we are washing our hands, using lots of soap.") When they are done, the child smiles and holds the doll.

What It Means

Young children often give clues about their interests. This teacher was able to interpret the nonverbal behavior of Erin and add to her play. Erin had a schema for diapering, which included the teacher's action of pushing up her sleeves before washing her hands. The teacher began with the actions Erin remembered, then added more actions, demonstrating each one and describing it with words. During this interaction, Erin's schema of diapering increased in detail and accuracy.

When we cannot find an existing schema in which to assimilate new information, we are uncomfortable and are in a state of *disequilibrium*. Because humans need to make sense of the world and need to find a place in our brains to store novel information, disequilibrium forces us to create a new place, a new schema. Just as we make accommodations for visitors to our home (we make a place for them), Piaget called making a new schema or reorganizing old schemas *accommodation*. Often this action of making new schema is a matter of breaking a big idea into smaller subparts that are linked together. For example, a child might start with a schema "food," and later break it into the linked categories of bread and vegetables, and still later break apart vegetables into the subcategories of fruits, legumes, leafy vegetables, and so forth. The new schemas are constructed by modifying the existing schemas. The new schemas create a more complex, inclusive, and accurate network of schemas for understanding the world.

Teachers often want to help when a child is confused, frustrated, or unable to understand something. But Piaget would say that the child's confusion can be a good thing, because it is likely to lead to accommodation of the child's schemas and, therefore, to cognitive development. Though unpleasant, this feeling of disequilibrium is a necessary part of adapting our ways of thinking to unexpected pieces of information about the world. The mental work of moving from disequilibrium to equilibrium is how we fine-tune our schemas, reorganize our schemas, and foster the development of increasingly complex thought.

Having Wonderful Ideas

A book about Piaget's theory had a terrific phrase in its title— "the having of wonderful ideas"—to describe the feelings children experience when their thinking abilities are growing (Duckworth 2006). That also describes what we can observe from the outside. A great early care and education program, therefore, is a place in which young children routinely have "ah-ha!" moments of delighted mental discovery.

Vygotsky's Theory of Socio-Cultural Development

Lev Vygotsky was a Russian psychologist whose work did not become known to Western psychologists until the first English translation appeared in 1962 (Vygotsky 1978, 1986). Like Piaget, Vygotsky believed that children construct their own knowledge through the interaction of experience with their existing beliefs and skills. In other ways, his conceptualization of development was different from anything Western psychologists had seen before. He proposed a theory of development occurring within social relationships rather than within the individual child. He proposed that a child's level of development was not just what the child currently knew, but also what was possible for the child to know or do while interacting with others. This represents a radical departure from the belief of most psychologists that mental development is a characteristic of the individual, which we should measure by testing the child alone.

Vygotsky was a brilliant scholar with degrees in many fields. Instead of identifying processes internal to each child as Piaget did, Vygotsky identified two aspects of cognitive development that reside not in the child, but in the community in which the child develops: language and social interaction. According to Vygotsky, five key processes help the child's cognitive development: the zone of proximal development, mentors, scaffolding, intersubjectivity, and private speech (Berk 2004). Each of these is a surprisingly useful idea for early childhood teachers.

Zone of Proximal Development

Vygotsky defined development as the next thing that the child could learn, know, or do with help. Thus, development is proximal, or very close, to what the child already knows or can do, and this development resides in the social world. He called this potential for learning the zone of proximal development (Vygotsky 1978; Berk and Winsler 2005).

For example, Kendra is a toddler who wants to pour milk from the quart jug into her cereal bowl. Her mother explains that she is not quite big enough to pour milk like grown-ups, but that Mom can teach a way to handle the big jug by herself. She tells Kendra to grip the handle of the jug with her right hand and place her left hand, her "helper hand," near the bottom of the jug. Then Mom helps her use her helper hand to steady the jug as she pours.

In this example, pouring from the jug is not something Kendra could do alone, but something within Kendra's zone of proximal development. This means that she could accomplish the action with help. Her mother provided both the social activity and language to help Kendra internalize the process of successfully pouring from a jug.

Scaffolding a Child's Performance

What We Saw

The teacher, Robin, sits with some toddlers using crayons. Randy complains, "I can't make a road." Robin asks him, "What does a road look like?" He answers, "Orange." "Find an orange crayon. Make a line," she tells him. He holds the crayon out to Robin, but she points to a line on the paper and tells him, "Take your crayon and follow that line. Okay, now follow this other line. Now you have your road." Randy looks at his paper and smiles. He gets another sheet of paper and different crayons and draws two parallel lines. "Look, I made a road!" Robin suggests getting a car to play on his road, and he does, asking, "Can I make another road?" Robin replies, "You can make as many roads as you like." He grins.

What It Means

At first, Randy could draw a road only with the help of his teacher, but following her assistance, he learns to draw a road independently. The ability to draw a road was in Randy's zone of proximal development. The teacher is his mentor, teaching Randy a strategy he can use in future drawing efforts. She encourages him to consider his concept of road ("What does a road look like?") and leads him through each step in drawing the road himself, but doesn't draw the road for him. Randy's pride in his new ability is evident in both his smile and his desire to repeat the new skill.

Expert Guides: Mentors

A mentor is anyone with skill greater than the child's with whom the child can perform at a higher level than when alone. Mentors are naturally in place for children wherever they live. They come in the form of parents, relatives, siblings, peers, teachers, and others the child meets along her developmental path. Vygotsky elevated this ubiquitous condition to a central part of cognitive development. Recall that for Vygotsky, development is not what the child already has learned, knows, or can do, but what the child potentially could do with help. Therefore, Vygotsky saw the role of mentor and guide as central to cognitive development. Put another way, Vygotsky saw development as inseparable from teachers.

Both formal and informal mentoring help children to learn, know, or do something they could not do by themselves. In the example of Kendra learning to pour milk from the pitcher, Kendra's mother was a mentor, providing expert assistance to help Kendra learn to do things she could not do on her own. Additionally, her mother used language to instruct Kendra, and also to make sure they were on the same page in terms of how they were going to pour the milk. Kendra and her mother used language to guide minor adjustments about the placement of Kendra's hands,

✔ Practice Tip

Playing with a Child

Most of this chapter's Practice Tips are about helping young children learn to solve problems or organize their thinking. But what about just playing? When there is no problem to solve, is there a cognitively stimulating way to play along with a child who is playing with dolls, building blocks, or playdough?

The top scientist to study children's play (Sutton-Smith 1974) offers this advice on when and how to play along with a child:

Observe

Begin by watching carefully for a while to see the child's interests and skill level.

Play Along

Join in the play at the same skill level as the child. Be careful not to impose a play level that is too complex and adult, as this may frustrate the child. For example, if a toddler is putting measuring cups inside each other, you can join in by doing the same.

Play a Little Above the Child's Level

After playing for a while at the child's level, you can introduce a slightly more complex play level. For example, you can turn the measuring cups over and place one on top of the other. Or pretend conversation between two dolls can be demonstrated by a parent after the child has mastered play with one doll. This is mentoring.

> ## Break Away and Observe Again
>
> After showing the child a new idea and arousing the child's interest, back away. Let the child practice and learn. You may be pleased with yourself for getting the child interested in a new idea, but resist the temptation to show the child something else right away. This could be a mistake. Before attending to another new idea, children need time to practice, to make their own mistakes, and to repeat a new action many times to make it their own. Wait until the new idea or skill is mastered. In some cases, this will take only minutes. In other cases, months may pass.
>
> If you or the child becomes impatient or bored with the "play-a-little-above" stage, then you should probably withdraw from the play situation. You may be trying to show the child too much. You shouldn't try to force learning when children are playing with creative materials. Above all else, children's play should be fun!

the rate of pouring, the amount to pour, and returning the jug to the table. Vygotsky called this the process of creating *intersubjectivity*. Through the back-and-forth of conversation, the social partners refine each other's understanding until they both have the same subjective experience.

Kendra's mother is a good teacher because too much support or too little support would have kept Kendra from learning so well. When mentors scaffold, they try to fill in the gaps in the child's ability. For instance, when teaching how to tie a shoe, we show the child the process and leave the last step, pulling the loop, for them to finish. Next, we have them do the last two steps, then the last three, and continue this way until they have mastered tying a shoe. Vygotsky believed scaffolding is an ongoing process found formally and informally in the company of mentors and peers.

Private Speech

Another important aspect of scaffolding is the way language transmits knowledge, and the way language moves from our outer, social world to become internalized in the cognitive structures of the child. When children talk to themselves, this is called "private speech" (Vygotsky 1978; Berk and Winsler 2005). Children talk aloud to themselves when working on difficult tasks and when trying new activities. Often this private speech was first learned in a social activity with a mentor. Kendra may talk to herself when pouring the milk next time, reminding herself (aloud) to use her helper hand or to pour more slowly. She may even use the same tone of voice as her mother did. In this way, children gradually become their own mentors. As cognitive development advances, private speech becomes internal and older children don't talk to themselves as frequently. However, remember that even adults use private speech on difficult tasks. For example, when confronted with difficult instructions (for example, putting a bookcase together), adults often revert to reading the directions aloud.

Social Deprivation

Because Vygotsky viewed development as taking place primarily within social interaction, where two or more people come to a common agreement about things (intersubjectivity), he believed children's play was a crucially important context for development. If Vygotsky is correct, then children raised with minimal human contact would be severely limited in not only their social development but also in their cognitive development. There are two fascinating case studies of exactly this: Genie (who was described earlier) and Victor, the "Wild Boy of Aveyron" (Lane and Pillard 1976).

The Wild Boy of Aveyron grew up in a forest in the southern part of France about 200 years ago, where he was discovered by hunters. From earlier sightings of him, and his lack of language and social skills, he was believed to have been abandoned as a very young child (Lane and Pillard 1976). A French psychologist, Jean Marc Itard, was pleased to discover the twelve-year-old and immediately began studying his abilities. After much testing and training, Itard found that he was able to neither socialize the boy nor teach him language. Without human mentors and guides early in life, he was unable to develop the cognitive foundations that allow us to learn, know, and behave as humans. This case study is consistent with Vygotsky's idea that children need to be imbedded in a social world that is rich with opportunities to interact with language.

PROMISING PRACTICE

Learning Logic through Everyday Questions

What We Saw

After putting a puzzle together, preschooler Tania announces, "It will be clean up time soon." Her teacher, Kelly, asks, "And then what will we do? Can we go outside today?" Another child answers, "No," and Kelly asks, "Why not?" The boy looks out the window. "Because it's raining." A third child, Aden, goes to the window to see if it is still raining. Kelly joins him and describes what she can see: "When I look outside, I see the cars have their window wipers going back and forth. What does that tell us? Yes, it's still raining out. So can we go outside?" "No," Aden answers.

What It Means

Kelly nurtures the children's thinking skills. When Tania shows her understanding of the daily schedule by predicting cleanup time, Kelly questions her knowledge of what comes next. She prompts the children to think about what activity usually comes next and to use their reasoning skills to understand the change of schedule. Kelly explains what she can see (windshield wipers) that helps her draw a conclusion about the rain. She is teaching the children to think logically.

Information Processing Theory

Information processing theory focuses on the mental processes of receiving information from the world, storing it, and retrieving it for later use (Munakata 2006). Unlike the other two theories, no one person is responsible for information processing theory. It has evolved from work over many decades that has led scientists to adopt a cognitive model (a model that includes internal thinking processes) in many different fields including, for example, computer science and economics. The process of receiving, storing, and retrieving information is the same for children as for adults.

Information processing theory shares some of the main ideas of Piaget and Vygotsky. Like the other two theories, it proposes that children play an active role in their own development, modifying their own schemas in response to direct experiences in the world. Like the other theories, this one has useful implications on how to improve the teaching of young children.

Figure 5.4 shows a simple version of the information processing model. This model represents the way perception, memory, and thinking seem to work. The parts of the model do not necessarily represent actual, physical locations in the brain, but rather abilities of the brain.

Figure 5.4

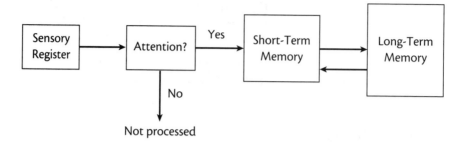

Sensory information comes first to our *sensory register,* which picks up any information arriving through our five senses (sight, hearing, taste, touch, smell). The sensory register holds that information for a very short time, less than a second (Sperling 1960), because humans are continuously bombarded with new information. An infant might sense music and human voices (auditory), the smells of food and people (olfactory), the taste of mother's milk (gustatory), the temperature of the room and the feeling of sucking (tactile), and the colors of the room (visual). William James once suggested that babies are born into "one great blooming, buzzing confusion" (James 1890, 488). So how does the sensory register filter all this information to prevent confusion? The answer is that it doesn't. The information passes through the sensory register, and only information we give attention to is processed. In information processing theory, "attention" is one of the keys to understanding what we perceive and therefore how we think.

Attending to the Senses

What We Saw

Amy, the teacher, takes Jaden, a toddler, by the hand in the play yard to show him something. She squats down and points to a spot in the grass. "See that? It's frost." Jaden looks closer, and Amy takes off his mitten so he can touch it. "Cold," he says looking at her. A classmate, Kathi, comes over and looks. Teacher Amy picks up a leaf and shows the children the frost on the leaf. "Is the leaf cold?" she asks, and Jaden touches it. Amy then points out more patches of frost on the grass. Later, Jaden picks up a leaf and shows it to Amy. "Frost," he says. Amy examines the leaf and says, "Look, the sun melted the frost, now it's just wet."

What It Means

Amy helps the children notice the wonders of the changing season. She aids Jaden's ability to take in information with his senses, make observations, draw a conclusion, and apply his understanding to another situation. She provides words for his experience to help him understand and remember what he has seen and felt.

Attention

In this theory, attention is that which the "mind's eye" is focused upon, the one piece of incoming information that has captured the interest of the child. Of all the sensory information described above, the newborn is probably most interested in the breast milk and suckling mom's breast. In this case, the attention is focused on sucking, swallowing, and tasting the breast milk. All the other information coming through the sensory register is essentially ignored, and therefore lost. Thus, we never really perceive most of the sensory input we receive.

Researchers find that some aspects of the environment are likely to capture our attention more than others. Our attention is most often captured by brightness, noise, movement, novelty, and self-relevance (Broadbent 1954). For example, everyone has had the experience of chatting at a social gathering. Suddenly, from across the room, you hear your name mentioned in another group's conversation. How were you able to pluck your name out of the din of conversation, apparently without even trying? Your attention was drawn to your name because we all care deeply about ourselves, and therefore, the information was self-relevant. In a word, the information was salient. This is such a strong and common research finding that researchers have dubbed it the "cocktail-party effect." Here are some of the other most common features of sensory inputs that make them salient.

Novelty

Children attend to sensory inputs that are new or changed (Baillegeron 1994). Once they get used to something, such as a sound or a picture, they stop attending to it. Change the input and it stands out from the array of incoming perceptions.

Brightness

Toys for children are colored with primary colors because they are bright (Berk 2005). The color doesn't matter so much as the brightness, because brightness is salient, drawing our attention. You can see for yourself by looking around the room you are in right now. What seems to draw your eye? The red pillow, the yellow poster, the noisy neighbors? Once you discover to what your attention (your mind's eye) is drawn, try *not* to attend to that one thing. After you have tried this and failed, you will understand salience!

PROMISING PRACTICE

Memory Games

What We Saw

As Rob, the teacher, gathers the two-year-olds for circle time, Chelsea asks if they can get out the feltboard bugs, and two other children echo the request. Even though he has not planned this activity, Rob gives an enthusiastic yes! and brings out the feltboard with the different pictures of ants, grasshoppers, bees, caterpillars, and other insects. After talking about the insects and naming them, the children begin their favorite memory game, "the bug in the rug." The children and teacher chant "Bug in the rug, bug in the rug, who's that bug in the rug?" Meanwhile, Rob turns the feltboard away from the children and covers one bug with a piece of felt. Turning around, he asks which bug has been covered by the rug. The children energetically shout their answers before Rob reveals the hidden bug.

What It Means

Rob changed his plan for rug time to follow the interest of the children. Children learn more when they are motivated by their own interests. Children attend most to things that act and move, which helps explain their attraction to crawling and flying insects. The sight of a bug moving tends to be a highly salient perceptual input, so children attend to it. Rob began by naming and describing each bug, which helps the children remember both the bug and its name, aiding recall during the game. Children love this and similar memory games because they challenge abilities that children are learning to exercise and perfect at this age: the abilities to focus their attention and recall information.

Movement

Our attention is always drawn to movement, and even infants pay attention to movement (Rovee-Collier 1999).

Self-relevance

Once children develop self-consciousness, they will attend to things that are self-relevant. This effect is likely to be stronger after the onset of self-consciousness at around fifteen to eighteen months (Bertenthal and Fischer 1978). But even before then, an infant's attention is likely to be drawn first to the photo she recognizes (for example, of her parents) out of all the photos in front of her. Self-relevance is the reason for the cocktail-party effect.

In summary, information that comes to the child must be attended to before it can be processed any further, and certain properties of information determine which will capture our attention.

Working Memory

Short-term, or working, memory is the next stage of information processing. Working memory can be thought of as a scratch pad where information is stored for a short period of time. Short-term memory can store about five to nine pieces of information and hold them there for a few seconds (Atkinson and Shiffrin 1968). Therefore, everything that gets into short-term memory does not necessarily get filed into long-term memory. Scientists have identified *control strategies* that people use to get information off the scratch pad of working memory and into long-term memory. This aspect of mental processing regulates the flow of information from the sensory register (all the sensations we might experience at the moment) to long-term memory. In addition, control strategies help us access information from long-term memory by helping people remember what has been stored.

One of the main control strategies is *rehearsal,* or what we usually call repetition. For example, when learning a new song, children need help in learning the words. Through repetition, the words move from short-term to long-term memory, until the children begin to recall the words the next day. Children like to learn things through repetition because the feeling of knowing something (remembering it correctly) is so rewarding.

Rehearsal

What We Saw

Holly, the teacher, finishes helping a child zip her coat and moves to the line of children waiting at the door. She says, "Hands in the air. Are there mittens?" The children raise their hands and respond, "Yes!" Holly taps her head and then her sides, "And a hat? And a coat? Are you ready?" The children copy Holly's actions and respond. Holly picks up on a conversation she just heard among the children. "What is this the first day of? Spring, yes? If there are big puddles outside, what should you do?" The response comes back, "Stay away." Holly continues, "If you heard the rule about puddles, raise your hand." All the children but one raise a hand. She asks that child if she heard the rule about puddles. She has. Holly leads the children outside.

What It Means

Holly uses a familiar ritual in a playful action chant to check that each child is properly outfitted for outdoor play. The daily repetition serves as a friendly reminder and last-minute check for the children, helping to signal that all are ready to leave for the play yard. Holly involves the children in thinking about and identifying in advance what to do in the case of puddles. She then checks to make sure each child has heard the rule. She is using the technique of rehearsal—reviewing their rules for dressing and puddles. This helps them move the dressing routine from working (short-term) memory to long-term memory. Therefore, they will be more likely to remember and comply with the rule.

Long-term memory is our complete store of knowledge. However, this store of knowledge is not just a large number of schemas, randomly scattered across the memory. Instead, it is a highly organized network of schemas in which schemas are connected to others in a hierarchical fashion. Broad categories exist in long-term memory, such as gender and animals. At the same time, the broad schemas are broken into subordinate schemas, such as the schemas for boys and girls under the heading of gender, and the schemas for dogs, and the schemas for every other kind of animal the child knows. The preschool years are crucial to cognitive development because this is when children construct this basic organization of their entire knowledge of the world. The number of developed schemas, as well as the quality of their organization, will affect the rate of intellectual development in the years to come (Griffen, Case, and Siegler 1994).

Children begin to form long-term memories based on large categories. The first long-term memories are of boundaries of high-contrast objects (Gwiazda and Birch 2001) and human faces (Mondloch et al. 1999; Johnson 1999). As children develop, they form categories in their thinking (schemas) that are more specific. For example, Cole, a toddler, has a dog named Yuba. When his family is driving, Cole points to other dogs and says "Yuba!" In fact, he even points at cows and says, "Yuba!" Yuba is his schema for all fury, four-legged animals. With time, he reserves the word "Yuba" only for dogs and eventually for only his family's dog. At the same time, Cole begins to create schemas for "cow" and "cat" and other four-legged animals. Eventually, he adds schemas at more specific levels (poodle, collie, terrier) and at more global levels (animal). When Cole is first confronted with a fox, he may need to think about whether it is a kind of dog (like a poodle) or whether it needs its own schema separate from dogs. In other words, is a fox a subtype of dog, or is a fox another animal like cats and goats? This is the kind of problem-solving that will lead to a more complexly organized store of knowledge.

Like the child's growing understanding of dogs and other animals, all of cognitive development can be described as a dual process of (1)

Figure 5.5

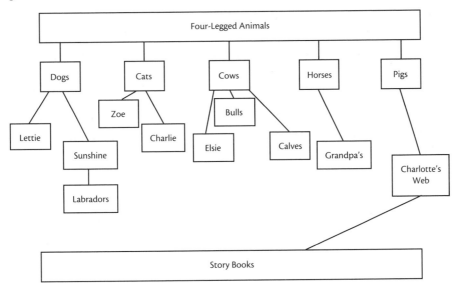

increasing differentiation (more and more specific categories) and (2) hierarchic integration (collecting schemas into logical, larger categories) (Werner 1948). Learning the words "poodle," "collie," and "terrier" is a differentiation process; learning that they are all part of the category "dogs" is the hierarchic integration process. Knowledge is not just a bunch of facts, but the way they are organized together. (See figure 5.5.)

ADDING NEW SCHEMAS

Early care and education programs give children countless opportunities to add new schemas to their knowledge base and to reorganize the schemas into better systems of categories. For example, the snack table might have slices of banana, orange, and kiwi. Michael, who has never seen a kiwi, can add it to his fruit schema. Linda, who is younger, might start to get the idea that all these tasty items are part of a single category called fruit. That's a big idea! A teacher can have fun with this. Hold out a rock and ask if it is a fruit. What about bread? What about carrots? Ask the children how they know if something is a fruit or not. After thinking this through together, the children will more easily be able to recognize (assimilate) as fruit any new fruits they have not tasted before.

Adult-Child Interactions That Stimulate Cognitive Development

The three theories of cognitive development provide an overview and general model of how the complexity and power of children's thinking grows. But what kinds of things can adults do to help that growth?

In Infancy

The infants who become the brightest children have adults in their lives who help them learn in the following ways (Belsky, Lerner, and Spanier 1984; Bornstein 2002):

- The adults are sensitively responsive to the child's needs. They pay attention to the child, asking themselves what the child must be feeling or thinking. They respond to the child with sensitivity and consistency. In other words, they form a secure attachment relationship with the infant (Riley et al. 2007).

- The adults generally accept the infant's exploratory behavior. They have made the home or early care and education center safe and clean so the infant can explore and learn about the world. Instead of spending long hours of the day in a crib or rocker, the most intelligent infants are given "floor freedom."

- The adults talk with the infant. In particular, they talk about what they are doing together or what the infant is experiencing (seeing, hearing, and so forth).

- The adults expose the infant in ongoing activities, such as shopping or cooking. One study found that babies who are held more on the hip or carried more in front packs learn more (Hunziker and Barr 1986). This is probably because they are more alert than other babies and are therefore exposed to more new sights and sounds.

MISTAKEN PRACTICE

Using Flash Cards or Videos to Build "Smart Babies"

Why It Doesn't Work

Young children learn best through real experiences and back-and-forth interactions with important people in their lives. According to Piaget, children learn by exploring the world—using their senses and growing motor control to manipulate objects and practice new skills. As Vygotsky explained, children learn from adults and others how to solve problems and complete tasks that they couldn't accomplish yet on their own. Children need exposure to real objects in order to develop verbal and mental labels and categories for these items.

Why It Happens

Parents want to do all they can to give their child a good start in life, and advertising convinces many parents they need to spend money to help their child learn. When parents are challenged to balance work and family, these products seem to offer a way to promote their child's success in the reduced time they have together. At the same time, teachers often feel pressure to provide "academic" curriculum for young children.

What Would Work Better

Make the most of the time spent with young children. Back-and-forth interactions between an adult and child are the key to promoting intellectual as well as emotional development. Provide a safe, interesting environment, and allow the child to explore with your guidance and encouragement. Make the most of daily routines such as diapering/toileting, mealtimes, and naptimes. Talk to children about what they are seeing, doing, experiencing, and feeling. Provide children with rich experiences: going to new places, cooking meals, playing simple games, reading books, and engaging in pretend play. These are the experiences that are essential for building connections in the brain, honing thinking and problem-solving abilities, and developing a meaningful understanding of the world.

Toddlers and Preschoolers

The young children who learn most easily have adults around them who use a particular style of interacting with them to solve problems. It is really a teaching style. This was first identified in research on mothers and their preschoolers. In a typical study, a parent would be asked to give her preschooler as much or as little help as he wanted in solving a difficult puzzle (Bee et al.1982; White 1988). Children who demonstrated the best outcomes in school a few years later had parents who engaged in the following behaviors:

- They let the child do it. They intruded less, allowing the child more time to work at his own pace. They didn't jump in impatiently to show the child the correct solution. They helped the child, but only when the child became frustrated and was about to quit.

- They gave general problem-solving advice. They were more likely to say things such as "Find the piece that fits in the corner" or "Try to find another red one" rather than "This one goes here." They gave their child a hint or a method rather than a solution. The child still had to solve the puzzle.

- Sometimes they would give the child direct instructions to get them re-involved in the activity. "Okay, start over here, and find a puzzle piece that has a straight edge." But then they would gradually withdraw their help, as the child showed interest and ability to finish the task on his own.

- They gave manageable tasks. Some tasks are too big or complex for a particular child. Good teachers know how to break a big task into smaller parts that are still challenging, but that the child can handle. For example, instead of just telling the child to wash the tricycle, a skilled teacher might start by listing all the steps (get out the equipment, wet the tricycle with the hose, scrub it with brushes, spray the soap off, dry it) and then go back to begin the first step. The child learns two things: how to wash a tricycle and how to break a big task into subparts so it is manageable.

- They gave advice in the form of questions. They would more often say, "Which puzzle piece is long like this?" rather than "This one is next." Questions challenge the child to think, and they teach the child what questions to ask himself when problem solving.

- They encouraged the child by telling him what he was doing right, not just wrong. They praised their children much more, rather than just pointing out the child's mistakes.

- They elaborated on the child's language. (See chapter 1.) If the child picked up a puzzle piece and said "Blue," the adult might expand on the child's language by saying, "Yes, it's light blue and shaped like a banana." The children heard many more words used to describe their experiences, and this increased their vocabularies, their understanding of many concepts, and their general memory abilities.

- They built on children's interests. They noticed when a child was interested in something and found ways to add to that interest. For example, if a child was interested in insects, the adult might find a picture book on insects, or an insect-collecting kit, or take the child to see an insect display at a museum.

Overall, the children who learn the most have teachers who do not give away the right answer too easily. These teachers pose problems that match the child's ability; they allow children to struggle with the problem and give additional hints and clues as needed. This encourages children to come face-to-face with any shortcomings in their own thinking and modify it accordingly, making them better equipped to solve the current problem and similar ones in the real world. Children carry this more complex and accurate thinking with them into the future.

Using Wisdom

Research shows that the most intelligent children have parents who expect them to do things for themselves (independence) and who let them struggle a bit on their own. These parents give help when needed, but don't intrude by solving the puzzle for the child. When their child is struggling to solve a puzzle or put on her jacket by herself, these parents give her the time to struggle, which is needed for competence to grow.

Consider the following report by a researcher who visited the Papago Tribe of Arizona in the 1930s (reported by Benedict 1938). She was sitting with several tribal elders of the Papagos, when the conversation was interrupted by ". . . the man of the house [who] turned to his little three-year-old granddaughter and asked her to close the door. The door was heavy and hard to shut. The child tried, but it did not move. Several times the grandfather repeated, 'Yes, close the door.' No one jumped to the child's assistance. No one took the responsibility away from her. On the other hand, there was no impatience, for after all the child was small. They sat gravely waiting till the child succeeded and her grandfather gravely thanked her."

Studies of Teaching Strategies

Researchers have also investigated the effectiveness of different teaching strategies in helping children learn (Mayer 2004). One way to summarize the findings is to think of three styles of teaching young children. The first style uses the traditional nursery school approach of discovery learning. These teachers prepare the classroom materials and activities carefully, then let children direct their own learning through their play. At the other extreme is the direct instruction approach, in which teachers tell children what to learn and help them through practice and drills. In between these two extremes is the guided learning approach, which blends some instructional guidance by the teacher with hands-on experiences by the child. Compared to the discovery learning approach, the guided learning approach also has more focused ideas about the learning objectives. For example, in chapter 3, we saw that children learn more from their experimentation with musical instruments if the teacher gives them some ideas of what to look for, such as changes in pitch or rhythm (these hints are called *cognitive advance organizers*) (Lawton and Johnson 1992). This whole book is, in a way, a promotion of the guided discovery approach. We aim to prepare early childhood teachers with the key concepts of our field so that they can more readily discover them in action during their interactions with children.

Guided Discovery

What We Saw

The teacher is working with a boy who is matching color tiles. He easily matches all the colors. The teacher then challenges him by setting out a green tile and asking, "What two colors make green?" He doesn't know. She gives him a hint that one is blue. He still can't figure out what the other one is. Then the teacher sets out a red tile and a white tile and asks what color he would have if he mixed those two together. He makes two guesses before saying pink. She takes him over to the easel and lets him try mixing the colors. First, he puts blue paint on the paper. Then he cleans his brush and adds yellow. As he brushes the yellow over the blue, the paper turns green right before his eyes! He is so excited he almost jumps into the air. Next, he tries red and white and again is thrilled by the transformation.

What It Means

The initial activity, matching color tiles, is too easy for this child. The teacher wants to give him a challenge, but the challenge she offers him turns out to be a little too great at first. This *matching of task difficulty with the cognitive abilities of the child* is the essence of great teaching. Recall the example from the beginning of the chapter where Dave gave Juan a puzzle that was slightly more difficult than he previously had solved. Psychologists have a lovely phrase for this: they call it a "delicate cognitive mismatch." With the paint example above, the teacher resists the temptation to tell the child the right answer. (Blue and yellow make green.) Instead, the teacher provides an activity in which the child can make the discovery himself. His excitement shows what a great job of guiding the discovery this teacher has done.

In several areas of research, the guided discovery approach has consistently provided the greatest learning. Researchers have studied topics as different as how to help children learn strategies for solving logical problems and how to help children learn to program a computer (Mayer 2004). All these studies converge on the same view, which has two key parts. First, children construct their own understandings through direct experiences with the world. Direct experience inevitably challenges their ideas (or schemas), which are forced to adapt, becoming ever more complex, integrated, and accurate representations of the world. We cannot fill a child up with knowledge the way we fill a glass with water, because memorizing facts does not improve the child's ways of thinking. The ability to think more complexly and accurately grows when children's preexisting ideas evolve through their efforts to resolve discrepancies between actual experiences and what they think or know. In this sense, children's knowledge is self-constructed.

The second key part involves the teacher's role. Teachers prepare the classroom environment and activities, and teachers challenge children with problems that force them to grow. In other words, the teacher guides the discovery.

Further Reading

On Research

Keil, F. 2006. Cognitive science and cognitive development. Vol. 2 of *Handbook of child psychology: Cognition, perception, and language.* 6th ed. Eds. W. Damon, R. M. Lerner, D. Kuhn, and R. S. Siegler, 609–635. New York: Wiley.

Munakata, Y. 2006. Information processing approaches to development. Vol. 2 of *Handbook of child psychology: Cognition, perception, and language.* 6th ed. Eds. W. Damon, R. M. Lerner, D. Kuhn, and R. S. Siegler, 426–463. New York: Wiley.

Nelson, C. A., K. M. Thomas, and M. de Haan. 2006. Neural bases of cognitive development. Vol. 2 of *Handbook of child psychology:*

Cognition, perception, and language. 6th ed. Eds. W. Damon, R. M. Lerner, D. Kuhn, and R. S. Siegler, 3–57. New York: Wiley.

On Practice

Berk, L. A., and A. Winsler. 1995. *Scaffolding children's learning: Vygotsky and early childhood education.* Washington D.C.: National Association for the Education of Young Children.

Chaille, C. 2007. *Constructivism across the curriculum in early childhood classrooms: Big ideas as inspiration.* Washington D.C.: National Association for the Education of Young Children.

DeVriew, R., and L. Kohlberg. 1987. *Constructivist early education: Overview and comparison with other programs.* Washington D.C.: National Association for the Education of Young Children.

Duckworth, E. 2006. *The having of wonderful ideas: And other essays on teaching and learning.* New York: Teachers College Press.

Kaltman, G.S. 2006. *More help for teachers of young children: 99 tips to promote intellectual development and creativity.* Thousand Oaks, CA: Corwin Press.

Tudge, J., and D. Caruso. 1988. Cooperative problem solving in the classroom: Enhancing young children's cognitive development. *Young Children* 44 (1): 46–52.

Children's Books (about clever children):

Bursik, R. 1992. *Amelia's fantastic flight.* New York: Henry Holt and Co.

Feiffer, J. 1998. *I lost my bear.* New York: Morrow.

French, S. 2002. *Guess the baby.* New York: Clarion Books.

Jonas, A. 1986. *Where can it be?* New York: Greenwillow Books.

Jonas, A. 1992. *The 13th clue.* New York: Greenwillow Books.

Lewis, T. P. 1984. *Mr. Sniff and the motel mystery.* New York: Harper and Row.

Lobel, A. 1982. *Ming Lo moves the mountain.* New York: Greenwillow Books.

Leuck, L. 1997. *My baby brother has ten tiny toes.* Morton Grove, IL: Whitman.

Mashiri, P. 1995. *The golden rain.* Braamfontein, South Africa: READ Educational Trust.

McKissack, P. C. 1986. *Flossie and the fox.* New York: Dial Books.

Nye, N. S. 2003. *Baby radar.* New York: Greenwillow Books.

Ormerod, J. 1998. *Who's whose?* New York: Lothrop, Lee, and Shephard.

Raskin, E. 1969. *And it rained.* New York: Antheneum.

Root, P. 1998. *One duck stuck.* Cambridge, MA: Candlewick Press.

Sharmat, M. W. 1987. *Nate the great and the boring beach bag.* New York: Coward-McCann.

Schwartz, A. 2003. *What James likes best.* New York: Atheneum.

Siddals, M. M. 1998. *Millions of snowflakes.* New York: Clarion.

Voake, C. 1986. *Tom's cat.* New York: Lippincott.

Wolff, P. R. 1995. *The toll-bridge troll.* San Diego: Harcourt Brace.

When Teachers Reflect: *Teaching by Creating Problems on Purpose*

Following Piaget, most theories of cognitive development have viewed intelligence as growing when it has to adapt to new situations. In other words, if your current way of thinking is good enough to solve every problem you encounter, then your thinking will not grow. Your intelligence grows when it has to, in order to adapt to a new situation or to solve a new problem.

If that is true, perhaps we could say that the role of a teacher is to create problems, to make life *less* comfortable for children!

- Maybe the best teacher brings three glue sticks to the table of four children, creating a problem they must solve.

- Maybe the best teacher brings out the shorter garden hose, which will not reach the garden, and lets the children figure out how to get water to the plants.

- Maybe the best teacher spots the problem of too many children wanting to use the class computer and calls a class meeting to ask the children how to solve the problem.

Of course, these teacher-created problems (such as the glue sticks and garden hose) or problems teachers avoid solving themselves (such as the crowded computer) will only lead to cognitive growth if the solutions are within the children's ability to solve. So not any problem will do. It has to be a problem that is only a tiny bit harder than the last one the children solved so that the adaptation they must make is small. Then they can succeed.

When Teachers Reflect: *Who Can Be a Mentor?*

Teachers should love Vygotsky's theory, because it emphasizes the important role of an expert (or mentor) from whom the child can learn. But think: who else in the classroom, besides the teacher, can be a mentor to the child?

In many classrooms, children learn from one another. One child can show another how to set the table for lunch. One child can show another the right way to put away the blocks. One child can show another how to use two hands ("use your helper hand") to pour milk without spilling. When the milk spills anyway, one child can show another where the bucket and sponges are and how to clean it up.

Making children into mentors for other children not only frees the teacher, but it is good for both children. We learn skills in a more complete way when we teach them to others.

On Monday, the teacher can show Paolo how to use the pencil sharpener. On Tuesday, Paolo can show Luisa how to use the sharpener. On Wednesday, when Oscar wants to know how to sharpen his pencil, the teacher has many options.

~~~~~~

When Teachers Reflect: Who Is Your Mentor?

Think about when you first started working with young children. You learned a lot in your first weeks and months. How did you learn?

You probably learned from your own experience, just seeing what worked and what didn't.

But, if you are like most teachers, you learned much of your skill from a more experienced teacher with whom you could observe and talk. Talk with successful professionals, in any profession, and you will find they can name mentors from whom they learned. Sometimes the mentors knew they were helping the person learn, and sometimes they didn't know. (They were being carefully observed without knowing it.)

Choose your mentors thoughtfully. When you find someone who you feel has much to teach you, find ways to be around that person. And remember to model "best practices" for those who follow you.

In the profession of early care and education, one of Vygotsky's most unusual claims is easy to see: knowledge exists primarily within social networks of people, not within individual brains. As you learn from your mentor, and you mentor others, the entire profession experiences a kind of collective cognitive development so that people entering the early care and education profession in the future will start out at a higher level of performance than we did.

When Teachers Reflect: *Does This Book Contribute to Cognitive Development?*

What would the theories of cognitive development say about this book? Should we expect this book to cause cognitive development in the reader? If it did, how would the theories explain it?

Piaget might say that the reader has existing schemas with which to understand the care and education of young children. This book, if it works right, will challenge existing schemas, requiring the reader to accommodate (modify) the schemas, perhaps even creating new ways of thinking.

Vygotsky might say that this book, if it works right, could function like a mentor, demonstrating advanced skills and understandings from which the reader could learn. Vygotsky might especially point to the Promising Practices throughout the chapters, in which the reader may observe many skilled teachers.

Information processing theory might predict that readers will attend to those parts of the book that are most salient to them, for example, parts that give them useful ideas for classroom issues with which they have been struggling. Once the reader attends to those parts of the book, information from the book will enter working memory and very possibly long-term memory, where the reader can retrieve the information later, back in the classroom.

In the end, we believe Piaget would remind us that, for this book to contribute to the development of the reader, the reader must use the information, reflect upon it, and *act* upon it. If the reader takes ideas from this book and "tries them out" in the real world of the early care and education classroom, then development is almost certain to follow, for both children and teacher.

Letter to Parents

Did You Know?

Because children's brains are not fully formed at birth, early experiences change the way the brain grows. Important structures in the brain continue to develop for the first several years. Stimulating early experiences, at home and in our early care and education program, can change the structure of the brain so that later learning is much easier.

Did You Know?

Scientists have compared children who received the intellectual stimulation of exceptional early care and education programs with similar children who did not. Those who receive stimulating experiences (likes the experiences we provide in our program) do better in later schooling and life. For example, they have higher IQs, complete their schooling more often, and own homes and have bank accounts more often as adults.

We Help Brains Grow

- We give children all kinds of problems to work on every day, such as figuring out how many cups we need at lunch or how to share two glue sticks between three children.

- Whenever possible, we let children figure things out themselves.

- We give hints and help when needed, but we don't solve the problem for the child. We want your child to become an independent problem-solver.

- We let children explore and experiment, and we give them ideas to help them see things in new ways.

- We teach them new words and new ideas every day.

- Researchers tell us that these kinds of "hands-on" experiences are the key to intellectual development in the preschool years. We provide child care, but we are also an *early childhood education* program.

From *Intellectual Development: Connecting Science and Practice in Early Childhood Settings* (Redleaf Press, 2009).

6

Why We Do What We Do for Children's Intellectual Development

Explaining Your Program Practices in Terms of State Early Learning Standards

What Are Early Learning Standards?

Most states are adopting "early learning standards," which describe the practices and outcomes they expect in early childhood settings. The design and implementation of these standards reflects an increasing appreciation by state and national policy makers that experiences in early childhood settings have a significant influence on future school success.

The design and implementation of state early learning standards is a fairly new development in the history of the early care and education field. Not all states have developed early learning standards yet, although it seems likely that each state will work towards that goal. To view the progress of individual states, visit http://nccic.acf.hhs.gov/pubs/goodstart/elgwebsites.html or contact your licensing agency, state department of education, or child care resource and referral agency.

Using Early Learning Standards

Early learning standards are not meant to function as a curriculum or an assessment. Rather, they are designed to provide a shared framework for understanding and communicating expectations for young children's development. Many state early learning standards align with curriculums such as High/Scope and the Creative Curriculum. For programs that do not use a formal curriculum, early learning standards can be a part of the teaching cycle by contributing consistency to the planning, implementation, and assessment of programming for children.

Early childhood professionals must be prepared to describe how their program meets state early learning standards through their curriculum, environments, and interactions with children. Although the standards are broken down into separate domains, they merge and overlap in practice. The categories are not intended to be rigid. For example, when we walk up stairs with children and count the stairs, we are not only laying the foundation for future mathematical learning such as one-to-one correspondence and sequencing, but we are also being mindful of health and safety needs such as holding onto the railing and approaches to learning by understanding that children learn through real-life experiences.

Must classroom environments and activities change to meet early learning standards? Perhaps not. Most quality programs already provide programming that meets the intent of these standards. The bigger challenge, which needs more attention, is in communicating developmentally appropriate practice and programming to others.

Communicating with parents and other stakeholders about your program helps them understand *why* you do *what* you do. Many parents do not always understand that, in early childhood, every moment is a teachable moment. The vast majority of learning is based on the child's own self-motivated actions along with our helping the child to reflect on those actions, not through worksheets, memorization, or group lessons. As a professional, you will need to teach parents and others how children learn every day through routines, purposeful activities, and interactions within a carefully constructed environment. You will also need to explain how the best early childhood settings look very different from later schooling environments. Here is where the language of your state's early learning standards can help you explain your program's philosophy, objectives, and strategies.

Your Professional Development and Early Learning Standards

Early learning guidelines help to define what children need to know, understand, and be able to do. The early learning standards may be state-wide; however, individual communities may use these standards as a common framework to address the unique needs and opportunities for children and families. *Core knowledge areas* and *core competencies* help to define what adults who work with children need to know, understand, and be able to do to support children in reaching desired outcomes. What this looks like will vary from community to community based upon the needs of the children and families, the resources of the community, and the partnerships involved.

So how does this affect your professional development? Early learning standards are becoming more influential in guiding the design of professional development systems. These systems help the staff of early care and education programs learn the core knowledge and core competencies (skills) for working effectively with young children. Increasingly, these core areas of knowledge and skill are based upon the professional needs and standards of the many kinds of programs in the birth-to-six service delivery system. Some states tie their early learning standards into a quality rating system that is used for subsidy programs for parents. Other states post the rating of child care programs in relation to how they meet their state standards. As you look at your professional development path, your state's set of early learning standards may be an important document that you use every day. For others, their state early learning standards may align with core knowledge areas and core competencies, which are tied into a registry system that tracks professional development experiences and assists in the planning of educational choices and directions.

Careers in Early Care and Education

The growth in numbers of specialized kinds of positions in the early care and education field has become quite remarkable and is another sign of the growing professionalization of the field. One state (Wisconsin) has put together a Career Guide that provides a wealth of knowledge about the types of jobs in early childhood education and the kinds of education and experience needed for each. You can view this career guide at www.collaboratingpartners.com/career_g/UnivTech.html. Find out if your state has a Career Guide and you may be surprised at how many options there are for employment in the early care and education profession. You may start in one kind of job, but prepare yourself to move into another. This was the case for all the authors of this book.

How Early Learning Standards Transition to K–12 Standards

Early learning standards differ from later academic standards in that early learning standards emphasize both the process and the content in each domain of learning. For example, because so much of early learning takes place within close relationships, children are more likely to learn their preliteracy or math skills, for example, within a secure, nurturing environment, where their social and emotional needs are also met. This emotional support is an essential part of the teaching-learning process. (We believe this is true of learning at every age, not just in early childhood, and the learning standards of later schooling are likely to reflect this principle more strongly in the future.) But the learning standards of early childhood and the K–12 school system ought to be coordinated so that the early childhood program prepares children for later success in school. This is one reason that alignment of early learning standards with K–12 standards is becoming more prevalent and makes a great deal of sense.

We often hear parents ask, "Will my child be ready for kindergarten?" A clear answer is difficult when different kindergarten classrooms have varying expectations of the children. This is where the alignment of early learning standards with K–12 standards can help facilitate smooth transitions from early care and education to later schooling. Many states have aligned their early learning standards with K–12 standards by using the same domains and language of that in the K–12 standards. Other states use the same domains and language in the early learning guidelines as the K–12 standards while adding domains more typically associated with younger children (for example, "approaches to learning" or "social-emotional").

When the early learning standards align with the K–12 standards, dialogue and understanding are facilitated between early childhood educators, K–12 staff, and parents. Some early childhood professionals may be concerned that this alignment represents a push downward of the elementary school curriculum. On the contrary, it ought to provide an avenue to educate each other and create better understanding between the two systems.

The National Association for the Education of Young Children (NAEYC) has a position statement on school readiness. When we refer to school readiness for young children, we are not only talking about children being ready for later school experiences; we are also talking about the readiness of school classrooms to be responsive in serving individual children. School readiness is a matter of goodness-of-fit between an individual child and a specific classroom. This approach uses a much wider lens to look at what it takes to foster successful learning. To learn more about school readiness you can visit the NAEYC Web site at www. naeyc.org/ece/critical/readiness.asp.

Additional Resources

Keeping abreast of trends and issues in the early care and education profession is helpful. One ongoing trend has been the increasing levels of accountability in areas such as assessment and outcomes. This takes us back to not only explaining *why* we do *what* we do, but it also beckons us to know the evidence that justifies our practices. Practices that are considered evidence-based are ones that have been demonstrated as effective within multiple research studies that document similar outcomes. This trend towards evidence-based practice is part of the professionalism of the early care and education field.

The field of early childhood special education has much to offer in this regard. The Division for Early Childhood (www.dec-sped.org) promotes policies and evidence-based practices that support families and enhance the optimal development of young children who have (or are at risk for) developmental delays and disabilities. Family and group child care programs are often the settings where parents and caregivers first notice and discuss the unique developmental patterns of children. But these same programs and caregivers often do not have adequate training in ongoing assessment, communication strategies, and referral processes to assist parents in getting help for their children.

Federal legislation such as the Americans with Disabilities Act (ADA) and the Individuals with Disabilities Education Act (IDEA) require that children and parents with disabilities must have an equal opportunity to participate in the child care programs and services in the least restrictive environment if a reasonable accommodation is possible. This means that more children with diagnosed disabilities may be attending early care and education programs as they receive support from early intervention specialists. Part of the role of these specialists is to facilitate learning opportunities that are embedded in the everyday activities of children. Regular communication and cooperation of caregivers with early intervention specialists about the strengths and goals of the child can really help. Early learning standards can be a very useful tool to guide this process. When early care and education and early childhood special education professionals become partners with parents, the children benefit. Take time to learn about the special education system for young children in your state or area.

The following is a sample of federal agencies, national organizations, and publications that provide information about strategies for including children with disabilities in child care settings.

Americans with Disabilities Act (ADA)

> Civil Rights Division, Disability Rights Section
> U.S. Department of Justice
> 800-514-0301
> www.ada.gov/ada

The ADA home page contains information about how to comply with ADA. ADA specialists are available to answer questions through a hotline. Services are also available in Spanish. This Web site contains information about ADA requirements, enforcement procedures, available technical assistance and materials, settlement information, the ADA Mediation Program, new or proposed regulations, and how to file complaints.

Learn the Signs. Act Early.

> National Center on Birth Defects and Developmental Disabilities (NCBDD)
> Centers for Disease Control and Prevention(CDC)
> www.cdc.gov/ncbddd/autism/actearly (English)
> www.cdc.gov/ncbddd/autism/actearly/spanish (Spanish)

Learn the Signs. Act Early. has information about childhood milestones and developmental screening and disabilities, including autism. An interactive tool allows parents to view how a developmental milestone category (social and emotional, cognitive, or language) changes as a child grows.

Most state early learning standards are designed to reflect the optimum growth and development of all children. Ongoing assessment of the children in your care (observing what abilities they have or lack) should ideally precede the planning and implementation of your program.

Table 6.1 summarizes the early learning standards for intellectual development from two states, and you may want to look at your own state standards for comparison. You will find that different language is often used across states. For example, some states avoid using the terminology of benchmarks; others use it as a primary focal point. Exploring the early learning standards of your state could be a productive activity for a staff meeting or an effective way to create a common ground of understanding in a community collaboration setting.

Table 6.1: Describing Your Program Practices in Terms of Early Learning Standards for Intellectual Development

Cognition and General Knowledge: Problem Solving			
Wisconsin Early Learning Standards (partial)	Washington Early Learning & Development Goals (partial)	WHAT you do	HOW and WHY it meets these standards
		Interactions	
• Applies problem-solving skills	• Problem solving	• Ask open-ended questions (for example, How could you . . . ? What are ways to . . . ?). • Find balance in allowing children time to solve their own situations without rushing in too soon or waiting too long, causing them frustration. • Model problem-solving actions and words for children.	• If an adult continually solves problems for children, children do not learn how to solve them on their own. Allowing children to become aware of a problem, test out possibilities, determine and evaluate solutions, develop reasoning skills, and use multiple strategies builds competence in this area. These strategies also build language and literacy skills.
		Environment	
		• Provide everyday household materials and toys (for example, blocks, cardboard boxes, props for dramatic play) that can be used in more than one way. • When something is new in the environment, ask children if they notice what is different.	• When adults are conscious of helping children view many solutions to a situation, the children become more flexible in their thinking and more adaptable and creative in their approaches to learning and acquiring knowledge.
		Curriculum	
		• Include games and puzzles in the curriculum to help a child work through problem solving by using color, shape, texture, contextual clues, and experience. • Look at your lesson plan. Do you intentionally create times for children to solve problems that meet their ability? Do you model problem solving for children in your classroom and with your coworkers?	• Problem solving is an approach that can be used throughout every part of the day, from transitions to mealtime to outside time. Try integrating problem-solving strategies in your lesson plan to see how often this skill is needed and used throughout the day. Music and art activities lend themselves very well to problem solving as children explore rhythms, test out patterns, mix colors, and explore a variety of mediums, using their senses.

Continued on page 196

Table 6.1 Continued

Cognition and General Knowledge: Critical and Analytical Thinking			
Wisconsin Early Learning Standards (partial)	Washington Early Learning & Development Goals (partial)	WHAT you do	HOW and WHY it meets these standards
		Interactions	
• Understands meanings as memory increases	• Children use past knowledge to build new knowledge	• Look for opportunities to make connections between previous experiences and current learning, talk about how children may have processed the experience through their senses of sight, sound, touch, taste, and smell. • Sing favorite songs and fingerplays with children, substituting the words to mirror their experience.	• The synaptic connections in the brain are continually growing and forging pathways that are related to experiences of the child. When children hear music, experience visual stimulation, and use their senses to engage in learning, they are building basic foundations for continued learning.
		Environment	
		• Provide toys and objects of different textures that respond to the actions of the child. • Use pictorial schedules in the classroom to help children remember the order of the day and also how things can change based on special events such as field trips, visitors, and so forth. • Use pictures in the classroom to capture learning experiences of the child and ways that learning can transfer to new situations.	• If a child has never seen a horse, or a picture of a horse, or heard a story about a horse, how would the child know what a horse is? It is our job as caregivers to expose children to a variety of experiences to help them learn about the diverse world we live in. It is always best to have children learn through their senses, and for us to be sensitive to individual and cultural differences.
		Curriculum	
		• Increase the complexity of stories, games, and other activities as the age or developmental level of the child progresses. • Play memory games with children by asking what they remember from yesterday, from last week, or from a particular experience. Write down their comments, create classroom books, and ask children what they are curious about.	• Ongoing assessment is an important component to looking at individual children and what they know and are able to do. Then you can plan your curriculum to meet the needs of children, challenge their growth and development, and engage in fun and meaningful learning.

Table 6.1 Continued

Cognition and General Knowledge: Scientific Thinking			
Wisconsin Early Learning Standards (partial)	Washington Early Learning & Development Goals (partial)	WHAT you do	HOW and WHY it meets these standards
		Interactions	
		• Follow the lead of the child as she explores the environment. • Ask the child questions ("Do you think they are the same? How are they different? Is one heavier than the other? Which one will sink?").	• Young children and their sense of wonder is a jewel to behold! When we nurture that sense of wonder with thoughtful questions, follow-up experiences, and respect for the process of inquiry, we help set the foundation for the child to develop an inquisitive mind and an openness to learning.
• Uses observation to gather information • Uses tools to gather information, compare observed objects, and seek answers to questons through active investigation	• Children collect information through observaton and manipulation	**Environment**	
		• Provide opportunities for safe observations and exploration. • Provide sensory materials for children to experiment with, such as water, sand, and playdough. • Ensure that children's outdoor experiences include a variety of settings to help them learn about the natural world.	• When we call attention to the details around our everyday living, we open up a wide world for children to experience. Observing the environment with all senses allows the preferred learning style of the child to be honored.
		Curriculum	
		• Small-group activities such as sink and float, magnetism, and cooking expose children to scientific concepts of measurement, comparison, and transformational change. (You mix flour, water, and yeast and get pizza crust!)	• When we are intentional about our curriculum choices based upon the age and developmental level of the child, we provide the basic language, experiences, and concepts that children need to be successful in scientific inquiry in the future.

Continued on page 198

Table 6.1 Continued

Cognition and General Knowledge: Mathematical Thinking			
Wisconsin Early Learning Standards (partial)	Washington Early Learning & Development Goals (partial)	WHAT you do	HOW and WHY it meets these standards
		Interactions	
		• Model using math and writing numerals in daily activities. • Talk aloud while doing simple math computations (such as counting the number of children for snack).	• We often think learning mathematical thinking is hard, so we avoid it. Changing our attitude toward mathematics can help young children learn basic concepts and be open to more complicated mathematical understanding.
		Environment	
• Understands number operatons and relationships	• Numbers and operations	• Provide a variety of objects for children to handle and manipulate (for example, buttons, pine cones, bears, stones). • Display numbers and operational signs (for example, the calendar, the number of children allowed in an area, the temperature inside or outside).	• Mathematical thinking is something we can infuse in our environment in a variety of ways. Sure, you can have a math area, but you can also be conscious of including math in your room arrangement and daily schedule.
		Curriculum	
		• Sing songs and read books with numbers and counting. • Provide opportunities for children to count objects during daily routines. • Provide a variety of materials that encourage counting, number recognition, one-to-one correspondence, and matching.	• Including a place on your lesson plan for mathematics can help you think about how to infuse these concepts throughout the day in a variety of activities.

Early learning standards address the "whole child" in an integrated manner. Therefore, by presenting only the learning standards for intellectual development, Table 6.1 provides only a partial view of the child.

The table summarizes performance standards from the state of Wisconsin and learning goals from the state of Washington in the areas of Cognition and General Knowledge, and explores them in terms of "What You Do" and "How and Why It Meets These Standards." The chart describes the interactions, environment, and curricula contributing to each of the standards, as covered in the chapters of this book.

To look for your state early learning standards, visit:

http://nccic.acf.hhs.gov/pubs/goodstart/elgwebsites.html or ask your licensing agency, state department of education, or child care resource and referral agency

The full set of Wisconsin Model Early Learning Standards can be found at:

www.collaboratingpartners.com/EarlyLS.htm

The Washington State Early Learning and Development Benchmarks can be found at:

www.k12.wa.us/EarlyLearning/pubdocs/EarlyLearningBenchmarks.pdf

Further Reading/References

Gronlund, G., and M. James. 2008. *Early learning standards and staff development: Best practices in the face of change.* Saint Paul, MN: Redleaf Press.

NAEYC. 2004. *Spotlight on young children and assessment.* Washington, D.C.: National Association for the Education of Young Children.

National Child Care Information Center. U.S. Department of Health and Human Services, the Administration for Children and Families: http://nccic.acf.hhs.gov/

References

Achilles, E. 1999. Creating music environments in early childhood programs. *Young Children* 54 (1): 21–26.

Anglin, J. M. 1993. Vocabulary development: A morphological analysis. *Monographs of the Society for Research in Child Development* 58 (10, Serial No. 238).

Antell, S. E., and D. P. Keating. 1983. Perception of numerical invariance in neonates. *Child Development* 54:695–701.

Atkinson, R. C., and R. M. Shiffrin. 1968. Human memory: A proposed system and its control processes. Vol. 2 of *The pyschology of learning and motivation*, eds. K. W. Spence and J. T. Spence, 742–775. New York: Academic Press.

Aylward, K., S. Hartley, T. Field, J. Greer, and N. Vega-Lahr. 1993. An art appreciation curriculum for preschool children. *Early Child Development and Care* 96:35–48.

Baillargeon, R. 1994. Physical reasoning in infancy. In *The cognitive neurosciences*, ed. M. S. Gazzaniga, 181–204. Cambridge, MA: MIT Press.

Bates, E., I. Bretherton, and L. Snyder. 1988. *From first words to grammar: Individual differences and dissociable mechanisms.* Cambridge, UK: Cambridge University Press.

Bee, H. L. 2000. *The developing child.* 9th ed. Boston: Allyn & Bacon.

Bee, H. L., K. E. Barnard, S. J. Eyres, C. A. Grey, M. A. Hammond, A. L. Speitz, C. Snyder, and B. Clark. 1982. Prediction of IQ and language skill from perinatal status, child performance, family characteristics, and mother-infant interaction. *Child Development* 53:1134–1156.

Beebe, B., D. Alson, J. Jaffe, S. Feldstein, and C. Crown. 1988. Vocal congruence in mother-infant play. *Journal of Psycholinguistic Research* 17:245–259.

Beilin, H., and E. G. Pearlman. 1991. Children's iconic realism: Object versus property realism. Vol. 2 of *Advances in child development and behavior,* ed. H. W. Reese, 73–111. Hillsdale, NJ: Erlbaum.

Belsky, J., R. M. Lerner, and G. B. Spanier. 1984. *The child in the family.* Reading, MA: Addison-Wesley Publishing.

Benedict, R. 1938. Continuities and discontinuities in cultural conditioning. *Psychiatry* 1:161–167.

Bergen, D., and J. Corcia. 2000. *Brain research and childhood education.* Olney, MD: ACEI

Bergeson, T. R., and S. E. Trehub. 2002. Absolute pitch and tempo in mothers' songs to infants. *Psychological Science* 13:71–74.

Berk, L. E. 2004. *Infants, children, and adolescents,* 5th ed. New York: Pearson Education Inc.

Berk, L. E., and A. Winsler. 1995. *Scaffolding children's learning: Vygotsky and early childhood education.* Washington, D.C.: National Association for the Education of Young Children.

Bertenthal, B. I., and K. W. Fischer. 1978. Development of self-recognition in the infant. *Developmental Psychology* 14:44–50.

Bleiker, C. A. 1999. The development of self through art: A case for early art education. *Art Education* 52 (3): 48–53.

Bornstein, M. H. 2002. Parenting infants. Vol. 1 of *Handbook of parenting: Children and parenting.* 2nd ed. Ed. M. H. Bornstein, 3–43. Mahwah, NJ: Erlbaum.

Bower, T. G. R. 1966. Stimulus variables determining space perception in infants. *Science* 149:88–89.

Bowker, J. E., and J. K. Sawyers. 1988. Influence of exposure on preschooler's art preferences. *Early Childhood Research Quarterly* 3:107–115.

Brazelton, T. B., B. Koslowski, and M. Main. 1974. The origins of reciprocity. In *The effects of the infant on its caregiver,* eds. M. Lewis and L. Rosembaum, 49–76. New York: Wiley Interscience.

Broadbent, D. E. 1954. The role of auditory localization in attention and memory span. *Journal of Experimental Psychology* 47:191–196.

Byrne, B., R. Fielding-Barnsley, and L. Ashley. 2000. Effects of preschool phoneme identity training after six years: Outcome level distinguished from rate of response. *Journal of Educational Psychology* 92:659–667.

Byrne, B., and R. Fielding-Barnsley. 1991. Evaluation of a program to teach phonemic awareness to young children. *Journal of Educational Psychology* 83:451–455.

Callaghan, T. C. 2000. Factors affecting children's graphic symbol use in the third year: Language, similarity and iconicity. *Cognitive Development* 15:185–214.

Campbell, F. A., E. P. Pungello, S. Miller-Johnson, M. Burchinal, and C. T. Ramey. 2001. The development of cognitive and academic abilities: Growth curves from an early childhood educational experiment. *Developmental Psychology* 17:231–242.

Campos, J. J., A. Langer, and A. Korwitz. 1970. Cardiac responses on the visual cliff in prelocomotor human infants. *Science* 170:196.

Chabris, C. F. 1999. Prelude or requiem for the "Mozart effect"? *Nature* 400:826–827.

Clements, D. H., and J. Sarama. 2000. Young children's ideas about geometric shapes. *Teaching Children Mathematics* 6:482–488.

Colker, L. J. 2005. *The cooking book: Fostering young children's learning and delight.* Washington, D.C.: National Association for the Education of Young Children.

Condry, J., and S. Condry. 1976. Sex differences: A study of the eye of the beholder. *Child Development* 47:812–819.

Cook, D. 1996. Mathematical sense making and role play in the nursery. *Early Child Development and Care* 121:55–66.

Cooper, R. P., and R. N. Aslin. 1990. Preference for infant-directed speech in the first month after birth. *Child Development* 61:1584–1595.

Copley, J. V. 2000. *The young child and mathematics.* Washington, D.C.: National Association the Education of Young Children and the National Council of Teachers of Mathematics, 18–23; 181–184.

Cox, M. V., and C. E. Parkin. 1986. Young children's human figure drawings: Cross sectional and longitudinal studies. *Educational Psychology* 6:1–38.

Colbert, C. 1997. Visual arts in the developmentally appropriate integrated curriculum. In *Integrated curriculum and developmentally appropriate practice: Birth to age eight*, eds. C. H. Hart and D. C. Burst, 201–223. Albany, NY: State University of New York Press.

Crncec, R., S. J. Wilson, and M. Prior. 2006. The cognitive and academic benefits of music to children: Facts and fiction. *Educational Psychology* 26:579–594.

Cronin, V., D. Farell, and M. Delaney. 1999. Environmental print and word reading. *Journal of Research in Reading* 22:271–282.

Daniels, M. 1994. Words more powerful than sound. *Sign Language Studies* 83:155–166.

Daniels, M. 1996. Seeing language: The effect over time of sign language on vocabulary development in early childhood education. *Child Study Journal* 26 (3): 193–208.

Davidson, L. 1985. Tonal structures of children's early songs. *Music Perception* 2:361–374.

DeCasper, A. J., and W. P. Fifer. 1980. Of human bonding: Newborns prefer their mothers' voices. *Science* 208:1174–1176.

DeHouwer, A. 1995. Bilingual language acquisition. In *Handbook of child language,* eds. P. Fletcher and B. MacWhinney, 219–250. Oxford, UK: Blackwell.

Dowling, W. J. 2001. Tonal structure and children's early learning of music. In *Generative processes in music: The psychology of performance, improvisation, and composition,* ed. J. A. Sloboda, 113–128. Oxford, UK: Clarendon Press.

Doxey, C., and C. Wright. 1990. An exploratory study of children's music ability. *Early Childhood Research Quarterly* 5:425–440.

Duckworth, E. 2006. *The having of wonderful ideas: And other essays on teaching and learning.* New York: Teachers College Press.

Dunn, L., S. A. Beach, and S. Kontos. 1994. Quality of the literacy environment in day care and children's development. *Journal of Research in Childhood Education* 9:24–34.

Edwards, C., L. Gandini, and G. Forman, eds. 1998. *The hundred languages of children: The Reggio Emilia approach—advanced reflections,* 2nd ed. Greenwich, CT: Ablex.

Fagan, J., and A. Iglesias. 1999. Father involvement program effects on fathers, father figures, and their Head Start children: A quasi-experimental study. *Early Childhood Research Quarterly* 14:243–269.

Fast, L. 1997. Artwork as an indicator of reading readiness in early primary grades: A preliminary study. *Canadian Review of Art Education* 24 (1): 33–45

Fenson, L., P. S. Dale, J. S. Resnick, E. Bates, D. J. Thal, and S. J. Petchick. 1994. Variability in early communicative development. *Monographs of the Society for Research in Child Development* 59:1–179.

Fernald, A. 1993. Approval and disapproval: Infant responsiveness to vocal affect in familiar and unfamiliar languages. *Child Development* 64:657–674.

Field, T. 1991. Quality infant day-care and grade school behavior and performance. *Child Development* 62:863–870.

Field, T. 1999. Music enhances sleep in preschool children. *Early Child Development and Care* 150:65–68.

Flavell, J. H. 1988. The development of children's knowledge about the mind: From cognitive connections to mental representations. In *Developing theories of mind*, eds. J. W. Arlington, P. L. Harris, and D. R. Olson, 244–271. New York: Cambridge University Press.

Forman, G. 2007. *Reflections on the Reggio Emilia approach: Different media, different languages*. Champaign, IL: ERIC/EECE Archive. http//: ceep.crc.uiuc.edu/eecearchive/books/regch4.html (accessed 11/10/07).

Forrai, K. 1997. The influence of music on the development of young children: Music research with children between 6 and 40 months. *Early Childhood Connections* 3:14–18.

Gardner, H. 1999. *Intelligence reframed: Multiple intelligences for the 21st century*. New York: Basic Books.

Gelman, R., and C. Gallistel. 1978. *The child's understanding of number*. Cambridge, MA: Harvard University Press.

Gelman, R., and E. Meck. 1983. Preschoolers' counting: Principles before skill. *Cognition* 13:343–359.

Geoghegan, N., and M. Mitchelmore. 1996. Possible effects of early childhood music on mathematical achievement. *Journal for Australian Research in Early Childhood Education* 1:57–64.

Ginsburg, H. P., A. Klein, and P. Starkey. 1998. The development of children's mathematical thinking: Connecting research with practice. Vol. 4 of *Handbook of child psychology*, volume eds. I. E. Sigel and K. A. Renninger, series ed. W. Damon, 401–476. New York: Wiley.

Golomb, C., and D. Farmer. 1983. Children's graphic planning strategies and early principles of spatial organization in drawing. *Studies in Art Education* 24 (2): 87–100.

Greene, D., and M. R. Lepper. 1974. Effects of extrinsic rewards on children's subsequent intrinsic interest. *Child Development* 45:1141–1145.

Griffin, S. A., R. Case, and R. S. Siegler. 1994. Rightstart: Providing the central conceptual prerequisites for first formal learning of arithmetic to students at risk for school failure. In *Classroom lessons: Integrating cognitive theory and classroom practice*, ed. K. McGilly, 24–29. Cambridge, MA: MIT Press.

Gromko, J. E., and A. S. Poorman. 1998. The effect of music training on preschoolers' spatial-temporal task performance. *Journal of Research in Music Education* 46:173–181.

Guthrie, P. J. 1994. The effects of development, manipulation of objects, and verbal cues on the spatial representation in young children's drawings. *Visual Arts Research* 20 (1): 50–61.

Gwiazda, J., and E. E. Birch. 2001. Perceptual development: Vision. In *Blackwell handbook of perception*, ed. E. B. Goldstein, 636–668. Oxford, UK: Blackwell.

Hakuta, K., and D. D'Andrea. 1992. Some properties of bilingual maintenance and loss in Mexican background high school students. *Applied Linguistics* 13:72–99.

Hallam, S., J. Price, and G. Katsarou. 2002. The effects of background music on primary school pupils' task performance. *Educational Studies* 28:111–122.

Hanes, J. M., and E. Weisman. 2000. Observing a child use drawing to find meaning. *Art Education* 53 (1): 6–11.

Hannibal, M. A. 1999. Young children's developing understanding of geometric shapes. *Teaching Children Mathematics* 5:353–357.

Hart, B., and T. R. Risley. 1995. *Meaningful differences in the everyday experience of young American children*. Baltimore, MD: Paul H. Brookes Publishing Company.

Hassler, M., N. Birbaumer, and A. Feil. 1985. Musical talent and visual-spatial abilities: A longitudinal study. *Psychology of Music* 13:99–113.

Hatfield, E., J. T. Cacioppo, and R. L. Rapson. 1994. *Emotional contagion: Studies in emotion and social interaction*. New York: Cambridge University Press.

Herberholz, B., and L. Hanson. 1995. *Early Childhood Art*, 5th ed. Madison, WI: Brown and Benchmark Publishers.

Hirsch, E. 1996. *The block book*. Washington D.C.: National Association for the Education of Young Children.

Hoff-Ginsburg, L. W. 1991. Mother-child conversation in different social classes and communicative settings. *Child Development* 62:782–796.

Hotchberg, J., and V. Brooks. 1962. Pictorial recognition as an unlearned ability: A study of one child's performance. *American Journal of Psychology* 73:624–628.

Howe, M. J. A., J. W. Davidson, D. G. Moore, and J. A. Sloboda. 1995. Are there early childhood signs of musical ability? *Psychology of Music* 23:162–176.

Hsu, H., and A. Fogel. 2001. Infant vocal development in a dynamic mother-infant communication system. *Infancy* 2:87–109.

Hunziker, A., and R. G. Barr. 1986. Increased carrying reduces infant crying: A randomized controlled trial. *Pediatrics* 77:641–648.

Huttenlocher, J., W. Haight, A. Bryk, M. Seltzer, and T. Lyons. 1991. Early vocabulary growth: Relation to language input and gender. *Developmental Psychology* 27:236–248.

Huttenlocher, J., N. C. Jordan, and S. C. Levine. 1994. A mental model for early arithmetic. *Journal of Experimental Psychology* 123:284–296.

Jalongo, M. R. 1996. Using recorded music with young children: A guide for nonmusicians. *Young Children* 51:6–14.

James, W. 1890, 1950. *The principles of psychology,* vol. 1. New York: Dover.

Johnson, M. H. 1999. Ontogenetic constraints on neural and behavioral plasticity: Evidence from imprinting and face processing. *Canadian Journal of Experimental Psychology* 55:77–90.

Kellman, J. 1994. The case for the developmentally appropriate lessons: The child and art. *Visual Arts Research* 20 (2): 62–68.

Kellogg, R. 1969. *Analyzing children's art.* Palo Alto, CA: Mayfield.

Kolbe, U. 1993. Co–player and co-artist: New roles for the adult in children's visual arts experiences. *Early Child Development and Care* 90:73–82.

Kontos, S. and L. Keyes. 1999. An ecobehavioral analysis of early childhood classrooms. *Early Childhood Research Quarterly* 14:35–50.

Krumhansl, C. L., and P. W. Jusczyk. 1990. Infants' perception of phrase structure in music. *Psychological Science* 1:70–73

Kuhl, P. K. 1994. Learning and representation in speech and language. *Current Opinion in Neurobiology* 4:812–822.

Kurtz, P. D., J. M. Gaudin, J. S. Wodarski, and P. T. Howling. 1993. Maltreatment and the school-aged child: School performance consequences. *Child Abuse and Neglect* 17:581–589.

Lamb, S. J., and A. H. Gregory. 1993. The relationship between music and reading in beginning readers. *Educational Psychology* 13:19–27.

Lane, H., and R. Pillard. 1976. *The wild boy of Aveyron.* Cambridge, MA: Harvard University Press.

Lawton, J. T., and A. Johnson. 1992. Effects of advance organizer instruction on preschool children's learning of musical concepts. *Bulletin of the Council for Research in Music Education* 111:35–48.

Leng, X., and G. L. Shaw. 1991. Toward a neural theory of higher brain function using music as a window. *Concepts in Neuroscience* 2:229–258.

Levin, I., and A. G. Bus. 2003. How is emergent writing based on drawing? Analyses of children's products and their sorting by children and mothers. *Developmental Psychology* 39:891–905.

Lomax, R. G., and L. M. McGee. 1987. Young children's concepts about print and reading: Toward a model of word reading acquisition. *Reading Research Quarterly* 22:237–256.

Lonigan, C. J., and G. J. Whitehurst. 1998. Relative efficacy of parent and teacher involvement in a shared-reading intervention for preschool children from low-income backgrounds. *Early Childhood Research Quarterly* 13:263–290.

Lonigan, C. J., S. R. Burgess, and J. L. Anthony. 2000. Development of emergent literacy and early reading skills in preschool children: Evidence from a latent-variable longitudinal study. *Developmental Psychology* 36:596–613.

Loveland, K. K., and J. G. Olley. 1979. The effect of external reward on interest and quality of task performance in children of high and low intrinsic motivation. *Child Development* 50:1207–1210.

Lowenthal, B. 1999. Effects of maltreatment and ways to promote children's resiliency. *Childhood Education* 75:204–209.

Lyytinen, P., M. Laakso, A. Poikkeus, and N. Rita. 1999. The development and predictive relations of play and language across the second year. *Scandinavian Journal of Psychology* 40:177–186.

Majsterek, D. J., D. N. Shorr, and V. Erion. 2000. Promoting early literacy through rhyme detection activities during Head Start circle-time. *Child Study Journal* 30:143–151.

Masataka, N. 1999. Preference for infant-directed signing in 2-day-old hearing infants of deaf parents. *Developmental Psychology* 35:1001–1005.

Matthews, J. 1994. Deep structures in children's art: Development and culture. *Visual Arts Research* 20:29–50.

Maxwell, L. E., and G. W. Evans. 2000. The effects of noise on preschool children's pre-reading skills. *Journal of Environmental Psychology* 20:91–97.

Mayer, R. E. 2004. Should there be a three-strikes rule against pure discovery learning? The case for guided methods of instruction. *American Psychologist* 59:14–19.

McKelvie, P., and J. Low. 2002. Listening to Mozart does not improve children's spatial abilty: Final curtains for the Mozart effect. *British Journal of Developmental Psychology* 20:241–258.

Mix, K. S., J. Huttenlocher, and S. C. Levine. 2002. Multiple cues for quantification in infancy: Is number one of them? *Psychological Bulletin* 128:278–294.

Mix, K. S., S. C. Levine, and J. Huttenlocher. 1999. Early fraction calculation ability. *Developmental Psychology* 35:164–174.

Mondloch, C. J., T. Lewis, D. R. Budreau, D. Maurer, J. L. Dannemiller, B. R. J. Stephens, and K. A. Kleiner-Gathercoal. 1999. Face perception during early infancy. *Psychological Sciences* 10:419–422.

Morrison, F. J., E. M. Griffith, and D. M. Alberts. 1997. Nature-nurture in the classroom: Entrance age, school readiness, and learning in children. *Developmental Psychology* 33:254–262.

Munakata, Y. 2006. Information processing approaches to development. Vol. 2 of *Handbook of child psychology: Cognition, perception, and language*. 6th ed. Eds. W. Damon, R. M. Lerner, D. Kuhn, and R. S. Siegler, 426–463. New York: Wiley.

Municipality of Reggio Emilia. 1997. *The hundred languages of children: Catalogue of the exhibit*. 2nd ed. Reggio Emilia, Italy: Reggio Children S. r. l.

Murray, A. D., and J. L. Yingling. 2000. Competence in language at 24 months: Relations with attachment security and home stimulation. *The Journal of Genetic Psychology* 161:133–140.

Murray, P. L., and R. E. Mayer. 1988. Preschool children's judgments of number magnitude. *Journal of Educational Psychology* 80:206–209.

National Institute of Child Health and Human Development—Early Child Care Research Network. 2000. The relation of child care to cognitive and language development. *Child Development* 71:960–980.

Nelson, C. A., K. M. Thomas, and M. de Haan. 2006. Neural bases of cognitive development. Vol. 2 of *Handbook of child psychology: Cognition, perception, and language*. 6th ed. Eds. W. Damon, R. M. Lerner, D. Kuhn, and R. S. Siegler, 3–57. New York: Wiley.

Nelson, K. 1973. Structure and strategy in learning to talk. *Monographs of the Society for Research in Child Development* 38:1–136.

Newland, L. A., L. A. Roggman, and L. K. Boyce. 2001. The development of social toy play and language in infancy. *Infant Behavior and Development* 24:1–25.

Newport, E. L., and R. P. Meier. 1985. The acquisition of American Sign Language. In *The cross-linguistic study of language acquisition*, ed. D. I. Slobin, 881–938. Hillsdale, NJ: Erlbaum.

Nichols, B. L., and A. S. Honig. 1995. The influence of an inservice music education program on young children's responses to music. *Early Child Development and Care* 113:19–29.

O'Neill, C. T., L. J. Trainor, and S. E. Trehub. 2001. Infants' responsiveness to fathers' singing. *Music Perception* 18:409–425.

Olson, R. K., and S. L. Boswell. 1976. Pictorial depth sensitivity in 2-year-old children. *Child Development* 47:1175–1178.

Parsons, M. J. 1987. *How we understand art: A cognitive developmental account of aesthetic experience.* Cambridge, UK: Cambridge University Press.

Paul, R. 1993. Patterns of development in late talkers: Preschool years. *Journal of Childhood Communication Disorders* 15:7–14.

Peery, J. C., and I. W. Peery. 1986. Effects of exposure to classical music on the musical preferences of preschool children. *Journal of Research in Music Education* 34:24–33.

Peisner-Feinberg, E. S., M. R. Burchinal, R. M. Clifford, M. L.Culkin, C. Howes, S. L. Kagan, and N. Yazejian. 2001. The relation of preschool child-care quality to children's cognitive and social developmental trajectories through second grade. *Child Development* 72:1534–1554.

Persellin, D. C. 1994. Effects of learning modalities on melodic and rhythmic retention and on vocal pitch-matching by preschool children. *Perceptual and Motor Skills* 78:1231–1234.

Peynircioglu, Z. F., A. Y. Durgunoglu, and B. Oney-Kusefuglu. 2002. Phonological awareness and musical aptitude. *Journal of Research in Reading* 25:68–80.

Piaget, J. 1950. *The psychology of intelligence.* Trans. M. Percy and D. Ellis. London: Routledge & Kegan Paul.

Piaget, J. 1952. *The origins of intelligence in children.* Trans. M. Cook. New York: International Universities Press.

Piaget, J. 1954. *The construction of reality in the child.* Trans. M. Cook. New York: Basic Books.

Piaget, J., and B. Inhelder. 1964. *The early growth of logic in the child: Classification and seriation.* Trans. E.A. Lunzer and D. Papert. London: Routledge & Kegan Paul.

Piaget, J., and B. Inhelder. 1973. *Memory and intelligence.* London: Routledge & Kegan Paul.

Pollak, S. D., and P. Sinha. 2002. Effects of early experience on children's recognition of facial displays of emotion. *Developmental Psychology* 38:784–791.

Rabitti, G. 2007. *Reflections on the Reggio Emilia approach: An integrated art approach in a preschool.* Champaign, IL: ERIC/EECE Archive. http://ceep.crc.uiuc.edu/eecearchive/books/reggio/regch6.html (accessed 11/10/07).

Rauscher, F. H., G. L. Shaw, and K. L. Ky. 1993. Music and spatial task performance. *Nature* 365:611.

Rauscher, F. H., G. L. Shaw, L. J. Levine, E. L. Wright, W. R. Dennis, and R. L. Newcomb. 1997. Music training causes long-term enhancement of preschool children's spatial-temporal reasoning. *Neurological Research* 19:2–8.

Rescorla, L. 1989. The language development survey: A screening tool for delayed language in toddlers. *Journal of Speech and Hearing Disorders* 54:587–599.

Rescorla, L., and E. Schwartz. 1990. Outcomes of specific expressive delay (SELD). *Applied Psycholinguistics* 11:393–408.

Reynolds, A. J., J. A. Temple, D. L. Robertson, and E. A. Mann. 2001. Long-term effects of an early childhood intervention on educational achievement and juvenile arrest. *Journal of the American Medical Association* 285 (18): 2339–2346.

Riley, D., R. R. San Juan, J. Klinkner, A. Rammingr, M. Carns, K. Burns, M. A. Roach, and C. Clark-Ericksen. 2007. *Social and emotional development: Connecting science and practice in early childhood settings.* Saint Paul, MN: Redleaf Press.

Ringgenberg, S. 2003. Music as a teaching tool: Creating story songs. *Young Children* 58 (5): 76–79.

Rosenthal, M. K. 1982. Vocal dialogues in the neonatal period. *Developmental Psychology* 18:17–21

Rovee-Collier, R. 1999. The development of infant memory. *Current Directions in Psychological Science* 8:80–85

Rymer, R. 1994. *Genie: A scientific tragedy.* London: HarperPerennial.

Sachs, J., B. Bard, and M. L. Johnson. 1981. Language learning with restricted input: Case studies of two hearing children of deaf parents. *Applied Psycholinguistics* 2:33–54.

Saxe, G. B., S. R. Guberman, and M. Gearhart. 1987. Social processes in early number development. *Monographs of the Society for Research in Child Development* 52 (2, serial no. 216).

Saxon, T. F., J. Colombo, E. L. Robinson, and J. E. Frick. 2000. Dyadic interaction profiles in infancy and preschool intelligence. *Journal of School Psychology* 38:9–25.

Schiller M. 1995. The importance of conversations about art with young children. *Visual Arts Research* 21 (1): 25–34.

Schweinhart, L. J., J. Montie, Z. Xiang, W. S. Barnett, C. R. Belfield, and M. Nores. 2005. Lifetime effects: The High/Scope Perry Preschool study through age 40. *Monographs of the High/Scope Educational Research Foundation* 14. Ypsilanti, MI: High/Scope Press.

Shonkoff, J. P., and D. A. Phillips. 2000. Communicating and learning. In *From neurons to neighborhoods: The science of early childhood development*, eds. J. P. Shonkoff and D.A. Phillips, 124–162. Washington, D.C.: National Academy Press.

Shonkoff, J. P., and D. A. Phillips, eds. 2000. *From neurons to neighborhoods: The science of early childhood development.* Washington, D.C.: National Academy Press.

Silverstein, Shel. 1974. *Where the sidewalk ends: The poems and drawings of Shel Silverstein.* New York: Harper & Row Publishers.

Sitton, R., and P. Light. 1992. Drawing to differentiate: Flexibility in young children's human figure drawings. *British Journal of Developmental Psychology* 10:25–33.

Sparling, J. J., and I. Lewis. 1984. *Learningames for threes and fours: A guide to adult/child play.* New York: Walker.

Sparling, J. J., and M. C. Sparling. 1981. How to talk to a scribbler. In *Exploring early childhood*, eds. M. Kaplan-Sarnoff and R. Yablans-Magid, 269–276. New York: Macmillan.

Sperling, G. 1960. The information available in brief visual presentations. *Psychological Monographs* 74: Whole no. 498.

Stannard, L., C. H. Wolfgang, I. Jones, and P. Phelps. 2001. A longitudinal study of the predictive relations among construction play and mathematical achievement. *Early Child Development and Care* 167:115–125.

Starkey, P., and A. Klein. 2000. Fostering parental support for children's mathematical development: An intervention with Head Start families. *Early Education and Development* 11:659–680.

Starkey, P., and R. G. Cooper. 1980. Perception of numbers by human infants. *Science* 210:1033–1035.

Starkey, P., and R. G. Cooper. 1995. The development of subitizing in young children. *British Journal of Developmental Psychology* 13:399–420.

Stevenson, H. W., and R. S. Newman. 1986. Long-term prediction of achievement and attitudes in mathematics and reading. *Child Development* 57:646–659.

Stipek, D. J., R. Feiler, P. Byler, R. Ryan, S. Milburn, and J. M. Salmon. 1998. Good beginnings: What difference does the program make in preparing young children for school? *Journal of Applied Developmental Psychology* 19:41–66.

Suthers, L. 2001. Toddler diary: A study of development and learning through music in the second year of life. *Early Child Development and Care* 171:21–32.

Sutton-Smith, B. 1974. *How to play with your child (and when not to).* New York: Hawthorn.

Tamis-Lemonda, C. S., M. H. Bornstein, and L. Baumwell. 2001. Maternal responsiveness and children's achievement of language milestones. *Child Development* 72:748–767.

Thompson, C. M. 1990. "I make a mark": The significance of talk in young children's artistic development. *Early Childhood Research Quarterly* 5:215–232.

Thompson, R. A. 2000. The legacy of early attachment. *Child Development* 71:145–152.

Tincoff, R., and P. W. Jusczyk. 1999. Some beginnings of word comprehension in 6-month-olds. *Psychological Science* 10:172–175.

Toomela, A. 2002 Drawing as a verbally mediated activity: A study of relationships between verbal, motor, and visuospatial skills and drawing in children. *International Journal of Behavioral Development* 26:234–247.

Trainor, L. J. 1996. Infant preferences for infant-directed versus non-infant-directed playsongs and lullabies. *Infant Behavior and Development* 19:83–92.

Trainor, L. J. 2002. Lullabies and playsongs: Why we sing to children. *Zero to Three* 23 (1): 31–34.

Trehub, S. E., D. Bull, and L. A. Thorpe. 1984. Infants' perception of melodies: The role of melodic contour. *Child Development* 55:821–830.

Trehub, S. E., D. Bull, L. A. Thorpe. 1985. Children's perception of familiar melodies: The role of intervals, contour, and key. *Psychomusicology* 5:39–48.

Trehub, S. E., A. M. Unyk, and J. L. Henderson. 1994. Children's songs to infant siblings: Parallels with speech. *Journal of Child Language* 21:735–744.

Trehub, S. E., A. M. Unyk, S. B. Kamenetsky, D. S. Hill, L. J. Trainor, J. L. Henderson, and M. Saraza. Mothers' and fathers' singing to infants. *Developmental Psychology* 33:500–507.

Trehub, S. E., and L. J. Trainor. 1998. Singing to infants: Lullabies and playsongs. *Advances in Infancy Research* 12:43–77.

Trehub, S. E. 2002. Mothers are musical mentors. *Zero to Three* 23 (1): 19–22.

Tudge, J., and F. Doucet. 2004. Early mathematics experiences: Observing young Black and White children's everyday activities. *Early Childhood Research Quarterly* 19:21–39.

Vondra, J. I., D. Barnett, and D. Cicchetti. 1990. Self concept, motivation, and competence among preschoolers from maltreating and comparison families. *Child Abuse and Neglect* 14:525–540.

Vygotsky, L. S. 1978. *Mind in Society: The development of higher psychological processes.* Cambridge, MA: MIT Press.

Vygotsky, L. S. 1986. *Thought and language.* Rev. ed. Cambridge, MA: MIT Press.

Warner, L. 1999. Self-esteem: A byproduct of quality classroom music. *Childhood Education* 76 (1): 19–23.

Wasik, B. 2001. Phonemic awareness and young children. *Childhood Education* 77:128–133.

Wasik, B. A., and M. A. Bond. 2001. Beyond the pages of a book: Interactive book reading and language development in preschool classrooms. *Journal of Educational Psychology* 93:243–250.

Weidner, C. G. 1998. Child art and the emergency of learning styles. *Visual Arts Research* 24 (1): 21–27.

Werner, H. 1948. *Comparative psychology of mental development.* Rev. ed. Chicago: Follett.

White, B. L. 1988. *Educating the infant and toddler.* Lexington, MA: Lexington Books.

White, B. L. 1990. *The first three years of life.* New York: Prentice-Hall.

Wigram, T., and C. Gold. 2006. Music therapy in the assessment and treatment of autistic spectrum disorder: clinical application and research evidence. *Child Care, Health, and Development* 32:535–542.

Winner, E. 2006. Development in the arts: Drawing and music. Vol. 2 of *Handbook of child psychology: Cognition, perception, and language,* 6th ed. Eds.W. Damon and R. M. Lerner, vol. eds. D. Kuhn and R. Siegler, 859–904. Hoboken NJ: Wiley.

Winsler, A., R. M. Díaz, L. Espinosa, and J. L. Rodríguez. 1999. When learning a second language does not mean losing the first: Bilingual language development in low-income, Spanish-speaking children attending bilingual preschool. *Child Development* 70:349–362.

Wolf, J. 1994. Singing with children is a cinch! *Young Children* 49:20–25.

Wolfgang, C., L. Stannard, and I. Jones. 2001. Block play performance among preschoolers as a predictor of later school achievement in mathematics. *Journal of Research in Childhood Education* 15:173–180.

Index

About the Authors

Dave Riley, PhD, began working as a Head Start assistant teacher in East Los Angeles in 1972. He has taught at the community college and university levels, spending the last two decades at the University of Wisconsin-Madison, where he is the Rothermel-Bascom Professor of Human Development and the associate dean for outreach of the School of Human Ecology. His published research has focused on early care and education, parent-child relations, and parenting education. He was the codirector of the Wisconsin Early Childhood Excellence Initiative and the Wisconsin Child Care Research Partnership.

Mary Carns has worked as an early childhood teacher, a movement teacher for preschoolers, and an observational data collector for child care research. Most recently, she has been employed as a research specialist at the Center for Genetic Medicine at Northwestern University. She has an MS in human development and family studies from the University of Wisconsin-Madison.

Ann Ramminger has over twenty-five years of experience as a teacher, an administrator, a trainer, and a consultant in various early care and education systems such as Head Start, full-day child care, part-day preschool, home visitation programs, and technical assistance organizations. Ann works with communities in Wisconsin on early childhood collaboration issues, such as four-year-old kindergarten and use of the Wisconsin Model Early Learning Standards. Recent projects include working on the revision to the Wisconsin Model Early Learning Standards and coordinating the early childhood component of a state professional development grant through the Waisman Center at University of Wisconsin-Madison. She has a BS in early childhood education from the University of Wisconsin-Madison and is working on an MS in administrative leadership with a concentration in adult and continuing education leadership.

Joan Klinkner has twenty years of experience working directly with young children, primarily in a teacher-training lab preschool at a community college. She has taught college courses in early childhood education and is currently an instructor at Northeast Wisconsin Technical College in Green Bay, Wisconsin. She is the author of numerous articles on child care issues, specializing in infant-toddler development and early childhood mentoring. She has an MS in early childhood education from Concordia University, in Saint Paul, Minnesota. She was the recipient of the Wisconsin Division for Early Childhood and Wisconsin Early Child-hood Association's Outstanding Service Award in 2005.

Colette Sisco has taught child development and other psychology courses at Madison Area Technical College since 1998. Before that, she taught psychology and human development courses and worked as an advising dean in the College of Letters and Sciences at the University of Wisconsin-Madison. She has an MS in psychology. Her graduate work specialized in social cognition and cognitive developmental psychology and included work on the effects of after-school programs on child development.

Kathleen Burns has six years of experience as an early childhood lead teacher. She also works as a teacher trainer and parent educator, primarily with at-risk families involved with the Kenosha County Division of Children and Family Services. She has served as a member of the Child Care Advisory Council for the Wisconsin state government and is a board member for the Kenosha Association for the Education of Young Children. She is also a "child care partner" on Kenosha County's Special Quest team that supports the inclusion of young children with special needs into early education settings by offering training and technical support. Kathy has a BA degree from Concordia University.

Cindy Clark-Ericksen has nine years of experience as an early childhood education teacher, including a year as head teacher of the High/Scope Demonstration Preschool in Ypsilanti, Michigan. She also has worked as the staff development coordinator and director of an early care and education program, as a community liaison for a four-year-old kindergarten program, and as a college instructor for courses in early childhood education. For eight years, she was the family living educator for the Cooperative Extension Service in her rural county. She has an MA in human development from Pacific Oaks College and an MS in marriage and family therapy from University of Wisconsin-Stout. She currently works as a family therapist.

Mary Roach, PhD, is the scientific director in the Department of Internal Medicine at the University of Wisconsin-Madison. She began her career as a preschool teacher, but has worked as a scientist for two decades, studying the quality of caregiver-child interaction as it relates to outcomes for children at risk for developmental delay, the role of families in supporting children's development, and the impact of public policies on the quality of early care and education. She was codirector of the Wisconsin Early Childhood Excellence Initiative and the Wisconsin Child Care Research Partnership.

Robert R. San Juan, PhD, has three years of experience as an early childhood educator. His research investigates young children's peer relationships, particularly the friendships of preschool-aged children. He has taught child development and parent-child relationship courses at the university level. Currently, he works as director of an outreach program at the University of Wisconsin-Madison that works with local nonprofit preschool programs that serve low-income children. The program helps foster preschoolers' school readiness skills, particularly language, early literacy, and social skills.